CONTENTS

REPEAT PATTERNS
a manual for designers, artists and architects

peter phillips +
gillian bunce

thames +
hudson

*Printed and bound in Slovenia by
Mladinska Knjiga*

Introduction   **PATTERNS ANCIENT AND MODERN**

Coral

Snowflake

The 'New Age' has seen an international resurgence of interest in the decorative arts. Design, as an issue, is high on the political as well as the cultural agenda. In a climate of constant change and enterprise, design and the designer have become very marketable commodities. Place the word 'designer' alongside any product and it gives it an immediate integrity and desirability. Descriptions such as 'designer clothes' and 'architect-designed' have become the catchphrases of our time. Design, however, can never just be seen as having an 'add-on' value, for it plays an integral role in the whole process, from the initial concept stage through development to manufacture and sales. In a modern technological culture, structure and order are particularly critical elements.

Now that societies are becoming ever more multi-cultural, there is a desire to see how patterns have been 'borrowed' and developed by successive cultures. This has led to an appreciation of the importance of design in contemporary society, and there is now a need to encourage learning by investigating the vital role that pattern structures play in ornamentation. Pattern links all cultures, through to modern technological society, and it also has a clear relationship with both the natural and manmade worlds.

However, there is a real danger that when art is copied from one culture to another it will lose its true significance, by failing to establish the meaningful social references that are necessary to give it integrity and relevance. Owen Jones, the 19th-century British architect and designer, believed in deriving inspiration from historical references, rather than imitating them, though, ironically, several of the illustrations from the *Grammar of Ornament* (1856) and many of his other works were copied directly by some of his contemporaries.

One of the most enduring motifs, known as the Paisley pattern, has united the cultures of the Eastern and Western hemispheres. Originating in pre-historic times as a representation of a plant form, it has been used continually, in various forms, for over two thousand years.

Paisley, 1680

Paisley, 1815

Paisley, 1990

When it was first introduced into Europe in the mid-18th century, the paisley pattern was interpreted as being very exotic. It was copied by many designers and used to great effect in the textile industries of Britain and France. The shawls that were the principal garments to be decorated with the motif remained an essential fashion statement for nearly a century, being adapted in size and shape to each new change in fashion.

Repeats have been used in ornament, decoration and design since antiquity. Repeating patterns can be traced from ancient and classical times through to the Gothic and Victorian periods, and culminating in the high-tech, computer-aided designs of today.

A pattern can be defined as a design composed of one or more motifs, multiplied and arranged in an orderly sequence, and a single motif as a unit with which the designer composes a pattern by repeating it at regular intervals over a surface. The motif itself is not a pattern, but it is used to create patterns, which will differ according to the organization of the motif. Examples of spiral patterns from draperies represented in Attic vase paintings are a good illustration of this.

The basic motif is the same in all three, but the arrangement differs, resulting in three completely different patterns. These patterns can be classified as follows:

by their historical and cultural origin, defined here as 'Attic', and their application, defined as 'draperies represented in vase paintings'

by the type of imagery used for the elements or motifs, defined here as 'spiral patterns'

by the organization of the motifs that form the structure of the patterns

This study of the language of repeats and their construction is an excellent starting point for the investigation of a subject that is fascinating to explore, and which can provide vital stimulus for the creative process. Construction plays an important part in the imaginative life of any pattern. It can be concealed, so that it acts in a subliminal way, as the eye moves from repeat to repeat without any awareness of a formal grid. However, visual stimulus can also be enhanced by allowing the repeat structure to dominate. Examples of this can be discovered in Chinese ornamentation, where the construction is both absolute and undisguised.

Repeat structures are a crucial element of pattern design, providing, as William Morris, a leading and influential member of the Arts and Crafts movement, stated: 'a wall against vagueness by means of definite form bounded by firm outline'.

Arts and Crafts movement design for ceiling paper, late 19th century

They constitute one method of organization used in many areas of design that are concerned with ornamentation. Such structures enable a design to be extended in any direction to create an uninterrupted pattern. Pattern is potentially infinite, and a well-designed pattern always gains by repetition. It must possess three essential qualities: beauty, imagination and order. Without the order that derives from successful repeating structures, neither beauty nor imagination can begin to be expressed.

Design exists not as a single motif/unit or picture that is merely reproduced, but as a continuous repeating pattern. This is most apparent when designing for fabrics, wallcoverings, laminates, carpets and tiles, where repeat is an integral part of the design and manufacturing process. However, it is also evident in many other art and design disciplines, from painting to architecture. Artists have always used geometrical principles and forms, recognizing the value of balance, harmony, geometrical precision and symmetry.

A realistic figure, linked in contiguous symmetrical series to create a repeating pattern

Many fine artists and graphic artists have been concerned with principles of harmony and order, from Leonardo da Vinci and Albrecht Dürer to the 20th-century Dutch graphic artist M.C. Escher. One of Escher's main preoccupations was the investigation and application of rules of symmetry to the plane. He was enormously fascinated by the production of multiple images, and this desire for multiplication can be seen in many of his works. Working from abstract geometric figures taken from Moorish mosaics and crystal formations, Escher developed innumerable realistic figures, which, when linked in contiguous symmetrical series, could be repeated to infinity. He fully appreciated the valuable contribution the Moors made to his understanding of shape and pattern, and the inspiration they gave him. The many brightly coloured, tile-covered walls and floors of the palace of the Alhambra in Granada and the Mezquita cathedral of Córdoba in Spain are excellent examples. Escher's work had many scientific and mathematical implications, and could be described as combining the unexpected with the inevitable.

The 1960s saw many artists, including Victor Vasarely, Andy Warhol and Bridget Riley, who used repetition as a means of conveying particular messages through their images. Andy Warhol's *Campbell's Soup Cans 200* (1962) created multiple representations to negate the 'significance' of the individual motif, and introduced mechanical processes to eliminate the 'preciousness' that is usually associated with the original artwork.

By contrast, the designer endeavours to transform the banal, obvious and static nature of repetition into pattern statements that have rhythm, harmony and an element of surprise; he or she attempts to keep the forms alive in spite of their endless repetition. One of the ways in which this can be achieved is through the understanding, use and manipulation of repeat organizations, which give movement, restore a sense of excitement and create the unexpected element that mass-produced, repetitive patterns require. In the series *Homage to the Hexagon* (1964-8), for example, Victor Vasarely produced work that employed repetition, structure and colour to create a dynamic sense of movement. The durability of a design derives from the knowledge that there exists potential for its recreation, manipulation and expansion.

The geometric structure of an Islamic pattern based on the hexagonal star, showing a construction method by compasses and rule

Number patterns were important to many early cultures and often had a powerful influence on their artistic development, particularly in the area of ornamentation. Two of the best-known number series to have had a great influence on design are the Vedic square and the Fibonacci series. The Vedic, or multiplication square is a pattern of numbers that forms the basis of a whole mathematical system, representing a numerical model of the universe. The Fibonacci number series is a more complex pattern source, which has held an enduring fascination for artists and mathematicians since its introduction into Europe in the early part of the 13th century. Leonardo Fibonacci of Pisa brought it to the attention of his contemporaries after studying mathematics with the Arabs.

Islamic architecture is a clear example of how mathematical systems and repeating number sequences can influence the ornamentation and construction of buildings. In the art of Islam, concept, number and pattern have always been closely interrelated, and have had an important influence on each other's development. This process of cross-fertilization means that a wealth of information may be stored within a simple pattern; the value of these rich layers of meaning may still be felt intuitively, long after their original function has been forgotten.

In Islam, illuminated script, metalwork, ceramics, textiles and architecture all express the same artistic vision and share a concern for pattern. Whether the decoration is on a scientific instrument, a carpet or a mosque, the layers of pattern, symbol and script offer a great depth of understanding. There is an interrelationship between the two-dimensional and the three-dimensional, and a sense of order is established through the integration of space, form and pattern.

Islamic harmonic growth pattern, demonstrating proportional increase to create illusions of space and movement

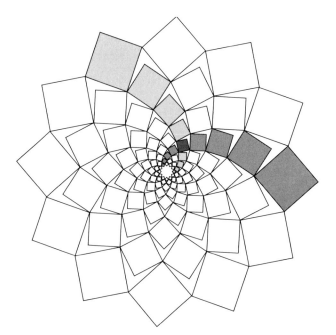

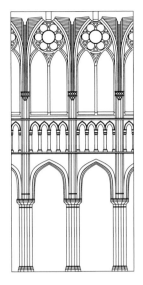

Elevation of the nave, Rheims cathedral, 13th century

In the Western world, the rib vaulting of the finest Gothic monuments, such as Durham cathedral and the chapter house of Wells cathedral in England, are impressive examples of how construction and repetition can create a dynamic and harmonic impact. The 13th-century naves of Rheims, Amiens and Cologne cathedrals and the nave vaults of Chartres cathedral show how concepts of form and pattern have been developed to a high level of complexity and aesthetic richness.

Walter Gropius, founder of the 20th-century Bauhaus movement, thought in terms of standardizing production, with functionalism and mathematical considerations being paramount. The Unité d'Habitation at Marseilles in France was one of his first architectural examples of the use of modular, standard repeating units. What he, like many other architects, created was a Warhol scenario applied to architecture.

China Wharf, designed by Piers Gough, one of the leading contemporary English architects, demonstrates a fresh awareness of ways in which architects can break the monotony of repetitive forms and the de-sensitizing nature of the conventional box. He creates complexity out of simple structures, constructing illusions of space and dimension.

Administration building for the Werkbund exhibition, Cologne, designed by Walter Gropius, 1914

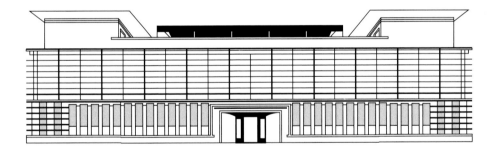

The importance of ornament in architecture has always been a contentious issue, and schools of thought have disagreed strongly about the value of its contribution. 'Modernism' considers ornamentation and decoration to be corrupt and meaningless, further exacerbated by repetition. At the turn of the 20th century the Austrian architect Adolf Loos wrote a paper entitled 'Ornament and Crime', in which he put forward the hypothesis that the more advanced and civilized society becomes, the more the psychological reasons for having decoration diminish. Opposing views are held by two leading contemporary Italian fashion designers, Giorgio Armani and Gianni Versace; the former believes firmly in the 'less is more' ethic, while Versace remains adamant that the less you have, the more boring the work becomes.

This is a very interesting area for debate and will always arouse strong passions. Clearly, though, great skill and a depth of understanding are required, whether the final solution is a very ornate or a simple statement. One of the great innovators of the 20th century, the German architect Mies van der Rohe, has perhaps best expressed this philosophy; 'God', he said, 'is in the details'.

The Victorian era witnessed an unprecedented increase in the use of surface ornamentation, especially in domestic decoration and textile design. From the 1830s onwards the newly established Schools of Design fostered an interest in all aspects of design; this was further encouraged by improved printing techniques, which made written material on the subject more widely available. It was also an era of eclecticism, and a great many of the books and articles produced on art and design at this time included sections on the origins of patterns and ornamentation, analyzing them in a historical and cultural perspective. There was also a great emphasis on the use of formal structure as an underlying framework for designs incorporating natural imagery. Historically, this can be seen as an expression of the cultural preoccupation with rationality in design and contemporary interest in the interrelationship of the arts and sciences. However, it can also be related to the production processes of the time.

In the case of printed textiles, this predominantly involved woodblock printing, in which the repeat size was limited by the size of a block that could be repeatedly lifted and placed by hand. When such a small repeat is in use the repeat structure is of crucial importance, as the eye will easily link a regularly repeated element in a pattern, creating lines of movement across it. The half drop repeat has traditionally been used to vary the linear movements in a repeated pattern, thereby visually increasing the width of the pattern.

The half drop repeat can be used to produce a visually non-directional design. Dresses of the 1930s were cut on the bias to give a 'floaty' effect, and the fashion fabrics for these dresses were mostly loosely drawn floral designs, half-dropped to give the impression of scattered flowers. Drops can also be used to emphasize directionality, the final effect being dependent on the scale and structure of the imagery in the repeat. The illustration on page 67, for example, shows the quarter drop used to give a strong diagonal. The accentuation or absence of direction and structure is one of the main factors that characterize changes in design styles. Furnishing prints of the late 1920s often had a strong horizontal direction, with the block and brick repeats being commonly used, and the 1960s geometric and 'ethnic' designs relied on the block repeat to define their regular structure. Over the last forty years, however, the ceramics, furniture and textile industries have undergone great technological changes. Developments in printing machinery have allowed for the production of larger designs, thus negating the practical importance of structured design.

Arts and Crafts printed textile design, 1902 (see page 61)

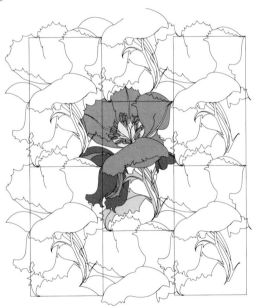

Today's 'quick response' ethos demands fast production and turnover of new designs. This has prompted the publication of many design source books. Some are reprints of 19th-century works by Owen Jones, M. Dupont-Auberville and others. These draw on designs from other cultures and eras, in which the structure is integral to the pattern. The character of the silk damask on page 51, for example, is defined as much by its 'classical' structure as by the imagery. But economic considerations now dictate that designs for fashion fabrics be relatively unstructured to allow for maximum utilization of the cloth when lay-planning (arranging the pattern pieces on the fabric). Also, most contemporary designs are produced in croquis, or sketch form and only put into repeat at the design conversion stage. Repeat is used here purely to create continuity, and the simplest repeat structures are therefore predominantly used.

Computers are now employed in many industries involved in design and production. In the area of printed textiles, the facility to specify various repeats of percentage drops and to create mirror images of individual motifs is often provided at the computer-aided design (CAD) and computer-aided manufacture (CAM) stages; the latter is catered for by computer-controlled laser engravers for rotary screens, laser film recorders for colour separations, and step and repeat machines of varying degrees of automation. The ability to visualize designs in repeat has been stressed as one of the benefits of CAD. As some designs produce strong diagonal movements when put into repeat, it is economically beneficial to be able to detect and correct this possibly undesirable effect at the design stage, rather than at the first production run.

There is now, in the computer graphics field, a wide range of software available for all types of computer, from the home computer through to the computer graphics workstation. Although the names of these individual software packages vary, they can be divided into two basic types: paint software and drawing software.

The main differences between these types are suggested by the names. Paint packages allow the user to work in a spontaneous, 'painterly' way. There are a variety of different 'tools', such as brushes and pens, and often different effects, such as chalk and watercolour. The aim is to simulate the effect of working with traditional painting and drawing media. Drawing software can be compared to technical drawing methods, in that the mathematical accuracy it permits allows for exact measurements. The drawing tools are usually limited to lines; these can form outlines of shapes, which can then be filled in. The parts of a design, or individual elements, can be individually selected, and then removed, edited, brought to the front or positioned behind other elements. Paint software provides a far more direct method of designing, but drawing software makes it easier for the user to make more accurate modifications to a design.

Both types of software provide functions that can be used to create repeating patterns. These are 'copy', 'move', 'mirror', 'rotate' and 'scale'. A method similar to the hand method described later (pages 17-20) can be used. A design unit is created, which can then be copied and moved. When drawing software is being used, this unit consists of a group of elements; in the case of paint software it is a rectangular section of the design area. Copies of the unit can be mirrored or rotated, and then placed in position. Drawing software allows the designer to specify the movement by measurement, and complex repeats can be built up by measuring the design unit and then calculating the distance to be moved. Certain paint packages provide grids that can be used to place the units with some accuracy. Specialist software packages for fashion and textile applications usually provide a limited range of repeat types, such as block, brick and various drops.

The repeat exercises and resulting patterns, supported by historical examples, that are provided in this book were created by combining repeat organizations and mathematical theories, which are inherent in the construction and analysis of pattern, with computer systems. Software is currently being developed that will allow the exercises and further pattern manipulation to be generated, and information to be stored with greater speed and efficiency.

The repeat systems help to explain, in visual terms, how a unit or motif can be developed through a series of repeat organizations to produce an infinite number of pattern variations. The establishment of a system where new ideas and possibilities are evolved creates that sense of excitement and expectancy which should be an intrinsic part of visual research and development. Analysis is then possible to determine how the resulting patterns can be further modified or extended, depending on how the units are exploited.

For the purpose of enhancing the visual impact, and to assist further development of a particular design, four other important elements – scale, texture, gradation and optical illusion – have been introduced. This helps to establish that understanding of a specific subject must be considered not in isolation, but in combination with other subject areas.

The complex and critical subject of colour, which is beyond the scope of this edition, is – together with repeat – an essential element that must be considered when developing ideas, as it can greatly affect the resulting pattern.

The illustrations in this publication were all produced on a Macintosh computer using the drawing package 'Aldus Freehand', which was selected because the mathematical accuracy of the software allowed very complex repeats to be constructed. This system proved ideal for assisting the creative process and generating an exciting range of pattern ideas. The computer makes designing a more immediate activity, where new ideas can be created, developed and modified at speed and at will. Changes of scale, line, texture, gradation, colour and distortion can be introduced in an extremely time- and cost-effective way.

If it is not possible to gain access to a computer and the relevant graphics software, similar results can still be achieved by more traditional means, as the same basic principles apply. Elementary equipment, which includes a ruler, scissors, glue and tracing paper, combined with plenty of patience and a photocopying machine, is all that the aspiring designer needs to carry out the exercises shown here. The following steps demonstrate how any original unit can be designed and used to create various patterns by the choice of different repeat organizations.

CREATING THE UNIT AND CONSTRUCTING THE REPEAT

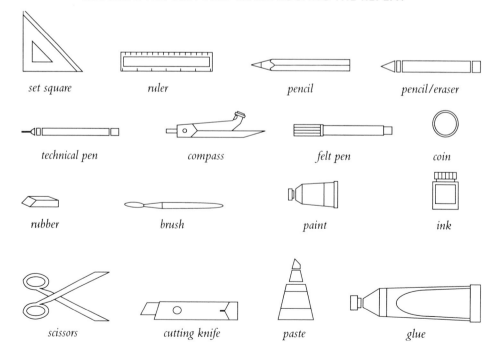

set square   ruler   pencil   pencil/eraser

technical pen   compass   felt pen   coin

rubber   brush   paint   ink

scissors   cutting knife   paste   glue

The unit can be drawn to any size, but to make effective and economical use of time and equipment when carrying out the exercises in this book, a rectangle in the ratio 2:3 with a 2cm grid is the most practical solution. This dimension enables the construction of a convenient size visually, and produces sufficient units to make maximum use of the space available on each A4 (29.7 by 21.0cm) sheet of paper. Other grids and paper sizes can, of course, be used.

Step 1   Construct a rectangle with sides in the ratio 2:3 (e.g. 4cm by 6cm).

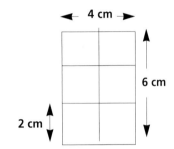

Equipment

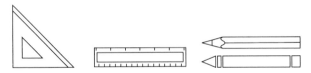

Step 2   Design an asymmetrical unit within the rectangle.

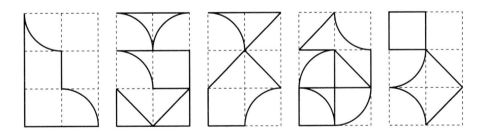

The design will be more effective as a repeating unit if it is asymmetrical, and if a combination of arcs, vertical, horizontal and diagonal lines, are incorporated.

Equipment

17

A coin can be used instead of a compass as a template to draw the arcs. Alternatively, if a less mechanical finish is desired, the arcs and lines can be drawn freehand.

Step 3

Creating multiples for reassembly. Construct a 2cm pencil grid on a sheet of paper.

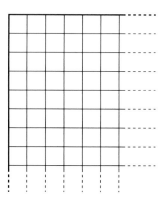

Step 4

a) Draft the unit onto the grid either by using geometrical instruments to draw out the entire area, or by using tracing paper to transfer the design. Note, though, that after using tracing paper several times, the line can become fainter, more crude and less accurate.

b) It is also necessary at this stage to create an additional sheet, so that a mirrored unit can be created.

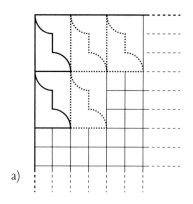 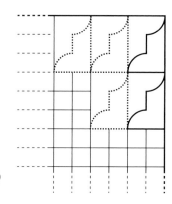

a)   b)

Equipment

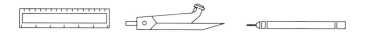

Step 5   Photocopy two sheets each of (a) and (b).

Step 6   Paint and fill in the positive and negative areas of the four photocopied sheets.

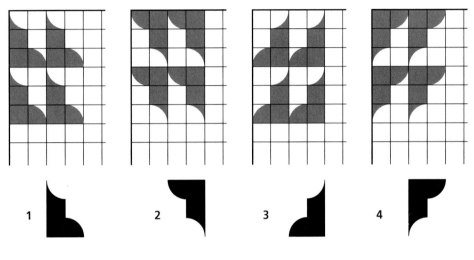

1   2   3   4

Equipment

Step 7   Photocopy as many of the four sheets as required to carry out the exercises described here and further experimentation. This may include the original photocopied line sheets.

Step 8   Cut the sheets up into single units.

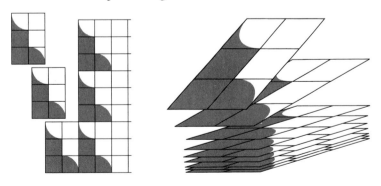

Equipment

Step 9 The units can be stuck down onto your chosen paper/card surface in any combination or permutation. The range of patterns can be infinitely varied, especially in a classroom/studio environment, where the creative impulse is allowed to express itself freely, and where designers and artists can develop their own methods of exploring their imaginative ideas.

Equipment

 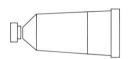

FURTHER DEVELOPMENTS AND APPLICATIONS

3D Illusions

Gradations

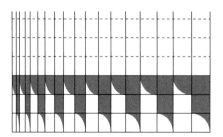

3D Constructions:
Surface Design

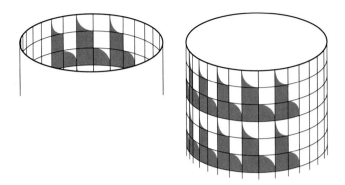

PROVING OR 'TESTING' A DESIGN

To visualize the pattern a particular design will create when it is repeated, it is necessary to reproduce it several times using one of the repeat organizations. In this way, all the edges and points at which the design repeats itself can be altered to fit exactly, and unwanted spaces filled in with relevant detail.

The example shown here is a brick repeat (page 85), but the same procedure can be followed for all repeats. It is necessary, for the purposes of this explanation, to assume that the original design is in croquis form (that is, a drawing of the design, not in repeat, but giving sufficient information to indicate how the final design will look).

Step 1

Fix the croquis to a flat surface with tape. Using a set square and ruler, draw a set of accurate guidelines, with cross-points, around the design to form a square or rectangle.

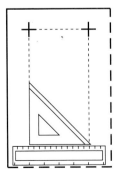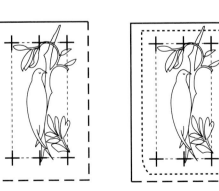

Step 1   *Step 2*

21

Step 2

Fix a large piece of good quality tracing paper centrally over the design and take an accurate tracing. The main outlines and shapes of the design should be mapped out in pencil at this stage. (If there are many intricate details in the design, these need not be included; this can be carried out at a later stage, once the structure of the pattern has been created). The cross-points are also traced from the original drawn rectangle.

Step 3

Remove the tracing paper and draw over the lines of the design on the reverse side with a pencil, so that it can then be 'rubbed' down the correct way round several times.

NB Too soft a pencil will create 'blurry' lines; too hard, and it will not leave sufficient lead on the surfaces to execute the required number of rubbings; the artwork will suffer as a consequence from a lack of definition. Rub the tracing through with either a sculptor's spatula or the handle of a spoon, or draw through with a pencil. Too sharp an instrument will make ridges in the paper, resulting in inaccurate copies.

Step 4

Take the tracing and place it on the desired paper surface. Then rub off the drawn area in the first and second positions. Ensure that the cross-points at the edges overlap exactly. If the guidelines do not line up, this indicates that the original rectangle was not drawn correctly.

Step 5

After removing the tracing from the second position, place it in the brick format below the two existing units.

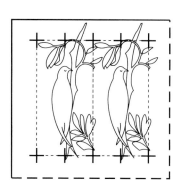

Step 4

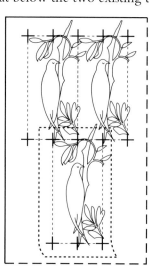

Step 5

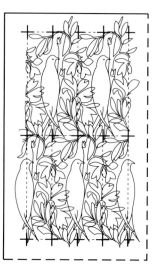

Step 8

Step 6

Repeat the procedure to complete the two remaining halves, in order to create a total of four units and enhance the clarity of the repeat organization.

Step 7

When the design has been repeated in this way, disjointed areas may become apparent at the points of repeat, where some shapes do not meet as they should. Some shapes may overlap at certain points and discordant shapes may clash and fail to be aesthetically pleasing. It may be necessary to reposition, adjust or remove some shapes altogether. When 'filling in' certain areas (if this is necessary), it is essential not to lose the character of the original design idea.

Step 8

Now that all the areas have been completed, the linear aspects of the design can be seen in a brick repeat. At this stage, having selected the correct working surface, additional detailing can be included before the design is coloured with the necessary media. This method of producing a design in repeat is the same, no matter which type of repeat is used; only the positioning of the tracing varies.

Repeat is an important consideration for the commercial designer, especially in the fashion and textile fields and many other surface design areas. It is one of the essential elements that invariably dictate whether the unit or motif will make a successful pattern, and consequently result in a commercially viable product. In a society that places great emphasis on 'market forces', anything that can assist in the success of a product must be valued. There are many equally important aspects that should be appreciated and understood, from colour and forecasting (trend information on colour palettes, yarn and fabric directions), to considerations of the type, quality, finish and handle of the materials employed. In the case of fashion fabrics, drape and movement also have to be part of the equation.

A better understanding of the principles of repetition, its significance and construction, is a major factor in creating good, innovative design. For the professional artist and commercial designer, this publication demonstrates how the use of repeats is not confined to one area, but has many applications. In education, it provides an introduction that will enable pupils and students at various levels of learning, and with differing degrees of experimentation and understanding, to become aware of how repeat can be used as a creative tool. The systems described here can be freely investigated by the amateur, or extended to high levels by more experienced artists, architects and designers.

THE SYMBOLS

The arrow and pattern units used in the diagrams and repeats

ROTATED UNITS:
(a) Basic unit
(b) 90 degrees
(c) 180 degrees
(d) 270 degrees

OUTLINE UNITS:
(e) Mirrored units
(f) Basic unit
(g) Horizontal mirror
(h) Vertical mirror

COUNTERCHANGED UNITS:
(i) Basic unit
(j) Counterchanged

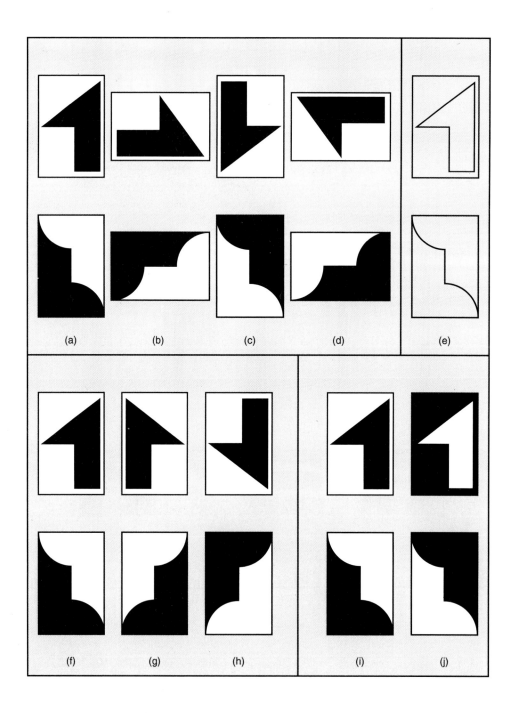

24

Chapter One

BLOCK REPEATS

The block repeat is the most fundamental of the repeat organizations. However, as in the case of the drop and brick repeat systems (pages 57 and 85, respectively), it permits the most comprehensive range of variations. The block can be mirrored (see page 39), thereby accentuating the static nature of the repeat, or rotated, which helps to create a design with more movement.

The most obvious and basic block repeat is that where the design block is positioned so that the design faces the same way at each repeat (for example, in the case of Andy Warhol's soup-cans). More complex designs can be created by rotating a block decorated with geometric patterns. If these are calculated carefully, designs can result in which the outlines of the basic block are disguised by the apparent complexity of the overall design.

The repeat can also be hidden by the use of an intricate and/or loosely structured design (see page 29).

BLOCK REPEATS

(a) Block repeat
Variations are produced
by introducing spacing
between the units:
(b) Pillar
(c) Stripe
(d) Open
(e) Diaper

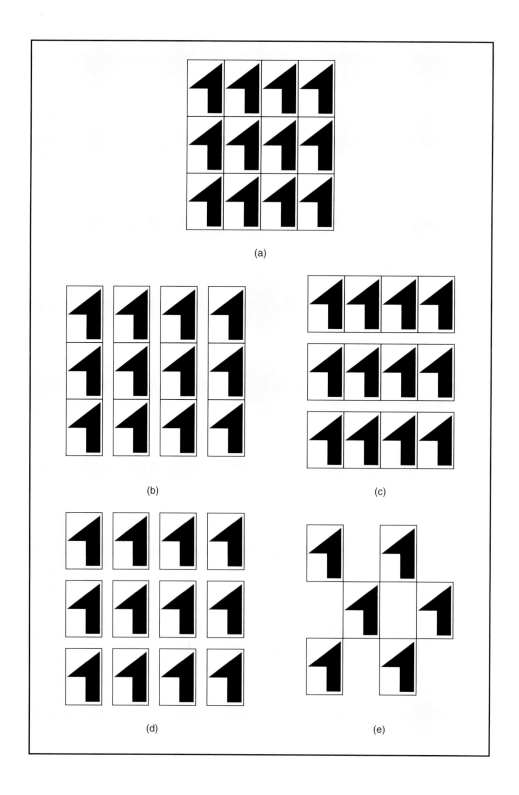

(a)

(b)

(c)

(d)

(e)

BLOCK REPEAT VARIANTS:

Left-hand column:

Horizontal mirror

Centre column:

Vertical mirror

Right-hand column:

Rotation

The altered units are
arranged in pillar
(a) to (c), stripe (d)
to (f), and diaper
organizations (g) to (i)

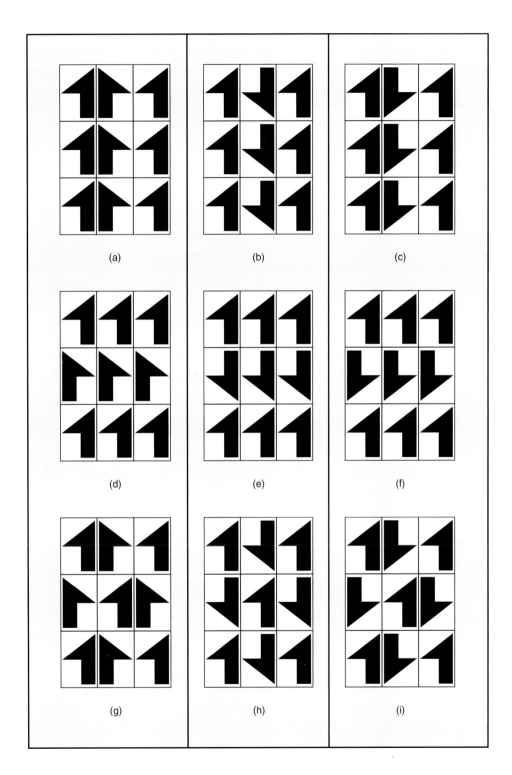

Block repeat

Branching stem pattern
from a cotton-printer's
woodblock. Indian,
19th century

Block pillar repeat

French lace-effect
design, 1988

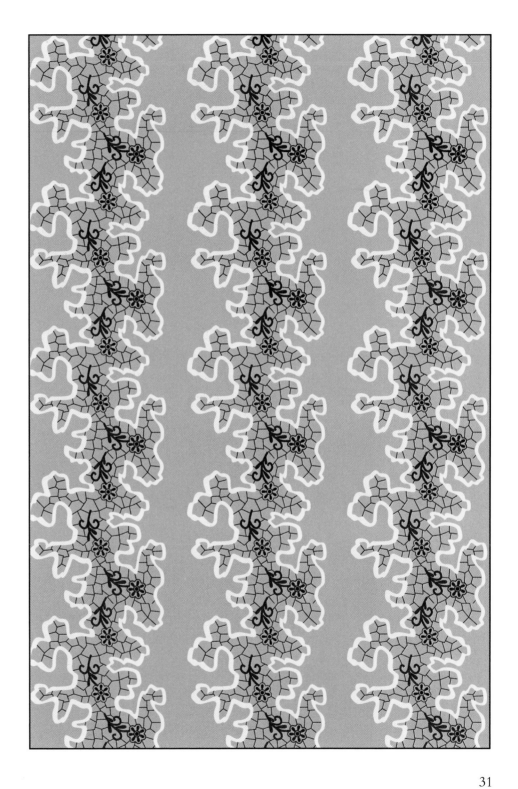

BLOCK REPEATS

Block stripe repeat

Textile design, 1950s

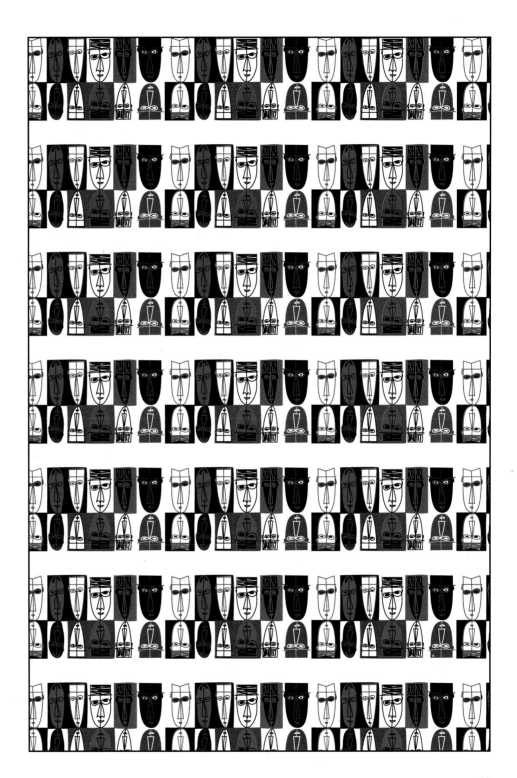

BLOCK REPEATS

Open block repeat

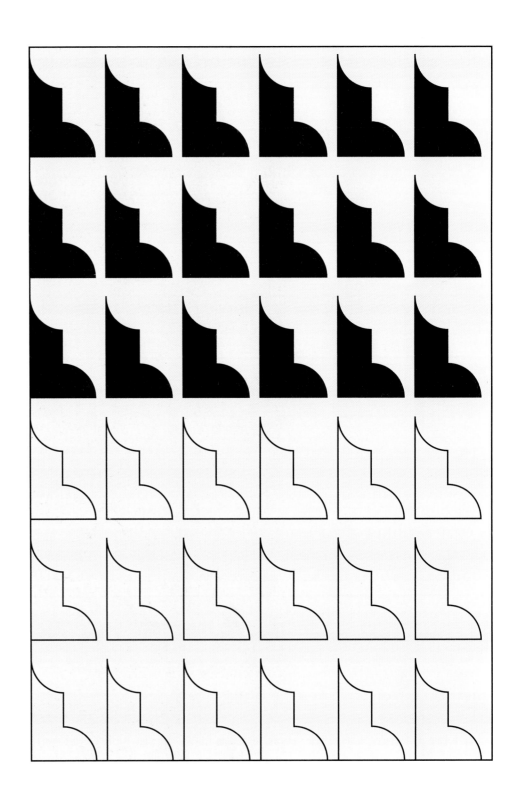

American Pop Art,
1960s

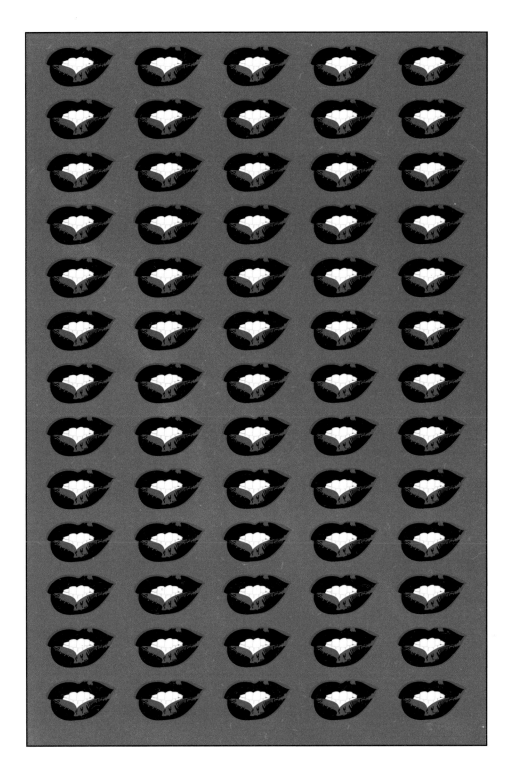

Block diaper repeat

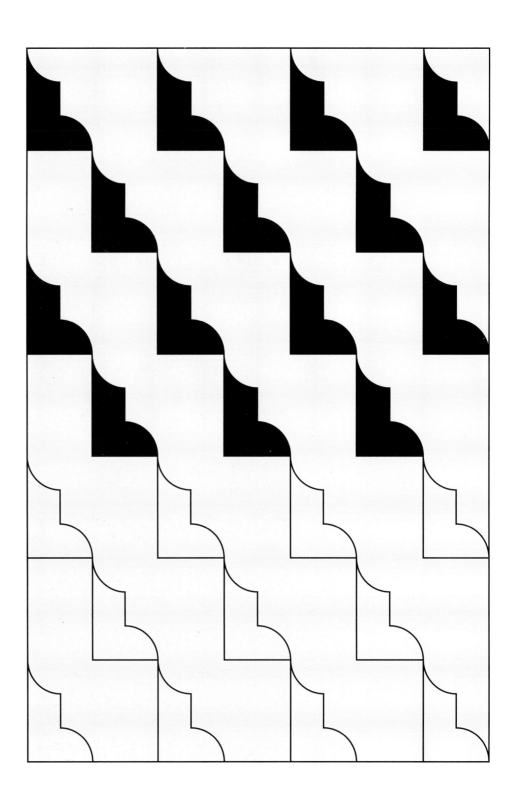

Indian woodblock
print, 19th century

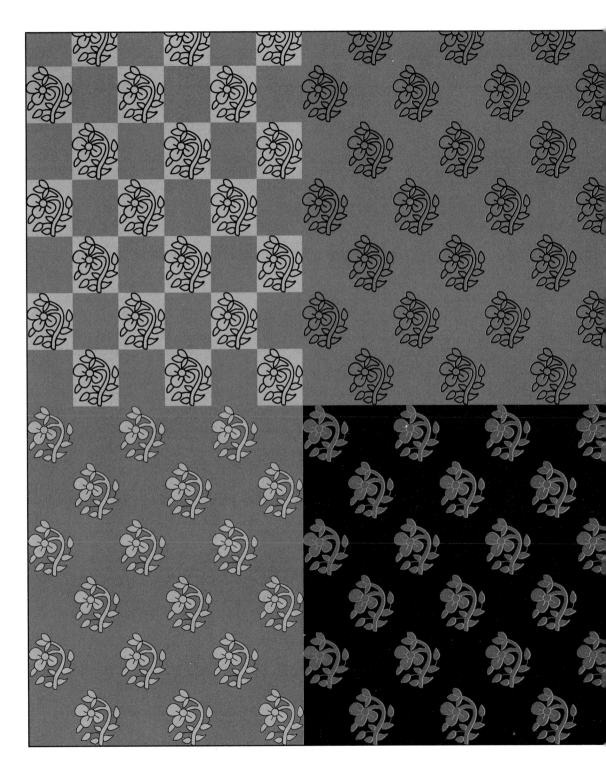

BLOCK REPEATS

Block repeat with
horizontal mirror,
pillar arrangement

Galleried house facade,
Spanish, late 18th
century

Block repeat with
vertical mirror,
pillar arrangement

Screen-printed textile,
1960s

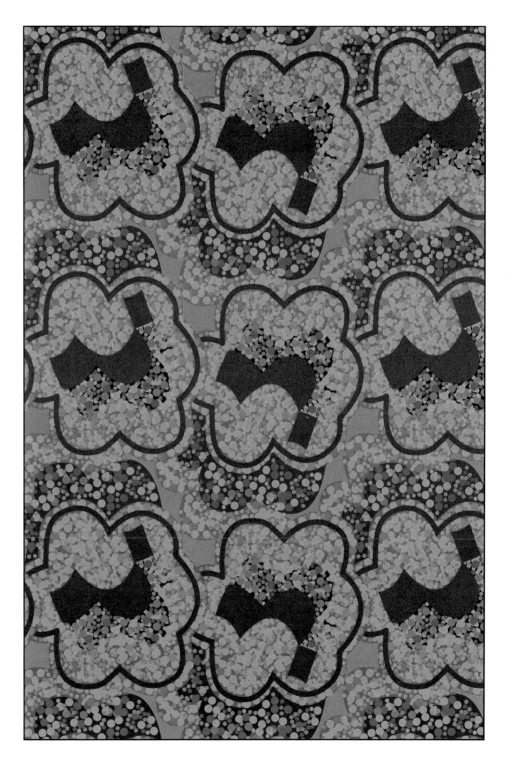

BLOCK REPEATS

Block repeat with
rotation, pillar
arrangement

Japanese textile design,
12th to 14th century

BLOCK REPEATS

Block repeat with
horizontal mirror,
stripe arrangement

Greetings card, 1991

Block repeat with
vertical mirror, stripe
arrangement

Dogtooth moulding,
12th-century cathedral
carving

BLOCK REPEATS

Block repeat with
rotation, stripe
arrangement

Right:
Greek marble mosaic
floor, 5th century BC
Below right:
Woven 'Sileh' carpet,
Caucasian, 19th century

BLOCK REPEATS

Block repeat with
horizontal mirror,
diaper arrangement

Italian silk damask,
14th century

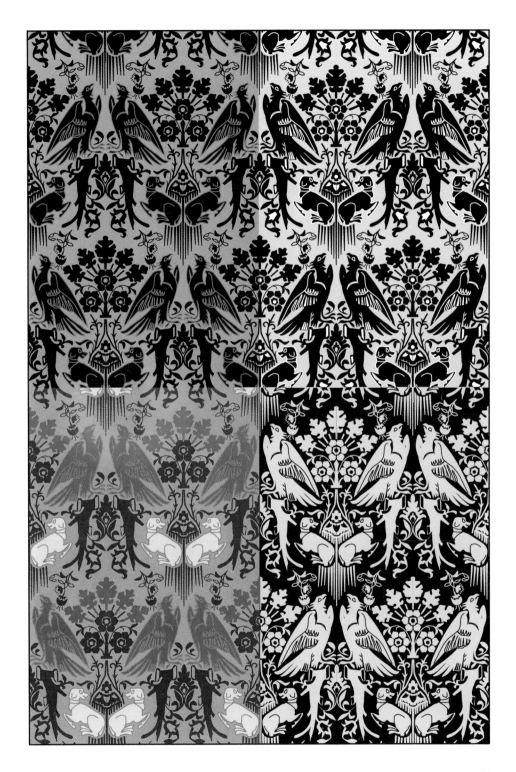

BLOCK REPEATS

Block repeat with
vertical mirror, diaper
arrangement

Right:
Chinese painted
porcelain vase,
19th century
Below right:
Chinese cloisonné
enamelled bowl,
19th century. The
main motifs appear in
this repeat, although
parts of the filling differ

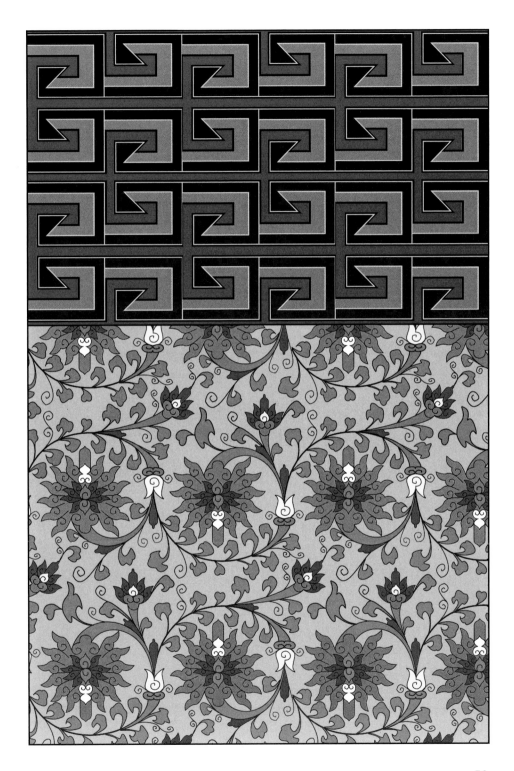

BLOCK REPEATS

Block repeat with
rotation, diaper
arrangement

French printed textile
design, 1800

Chapter Two   DROP REPEATS

The half drop repeat is perhaps the most commonly found of all the repeat systems; it is widely used in the wallcovering industry, where it helps to increase visually the width of a pattern. The repeat is derived by positioning each unit half-way down the next unit. It is possible to use quarter drops and other fractional drops, to create either a gradual or a steeply stepped arrangement, according to the effect required.

Depending on the scale and structure of the imagery in the design, drops can be used to create diaper effects (see opposite), strong diagonals (page 67) or a relatively random appearance (page 183). Mirroring can produce zig-zag or serpentine effects (pages 73 and 75), which can be further accentuated by the use of diagonal lines.

DROP REPEATS:

(a) Half drop

(b) Step

(c) One-third drop

(d) Quarter drop

Spacing introduced to (a) produces (e) Half drop pillar, and (f) Open half drop

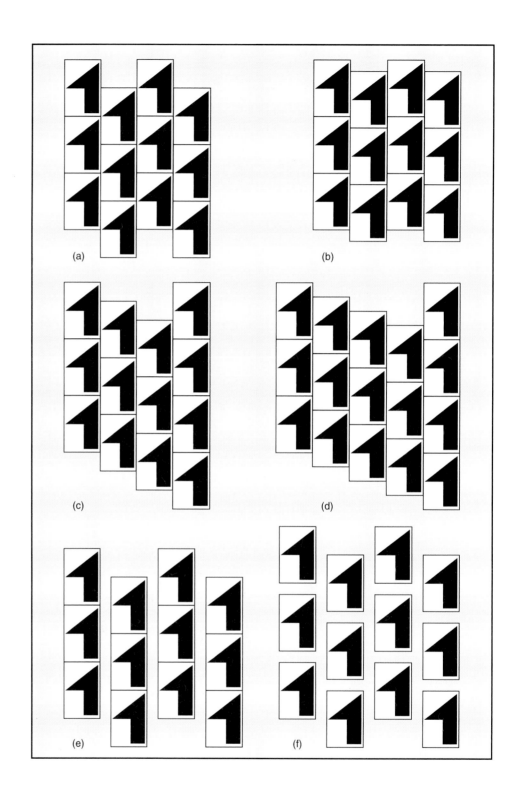

DROP REPEAT VARIANTS:

Top row:

Horizontal mirror

Centre row:

Vertical mirror

Bottom row:

Rotation

(a) to (c) are pillar
arrangements,

(d) to (f) are striped.

They can be used in
any of the drop repeat
arrangements shown on
the page opposite

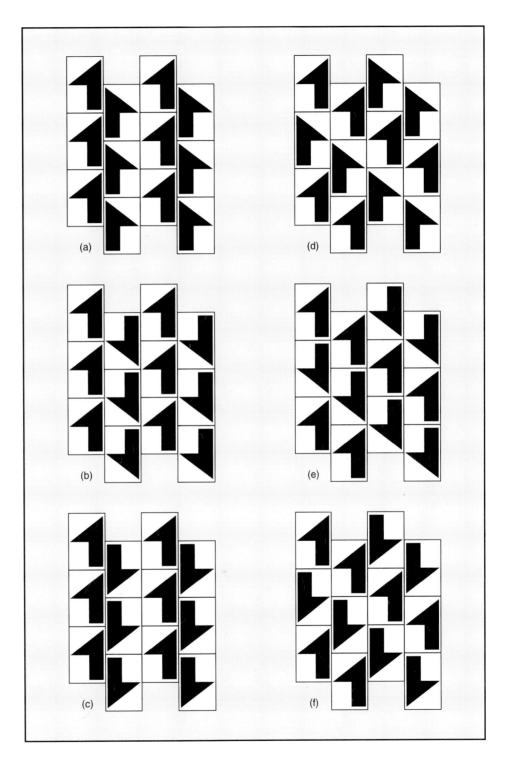

DROP REPEATS

Half drop repeat

Arts and Crafts printed
textile design, 1902

DROP REPEATS

Step repeat

Chinese painted bottle,
mid–18th century

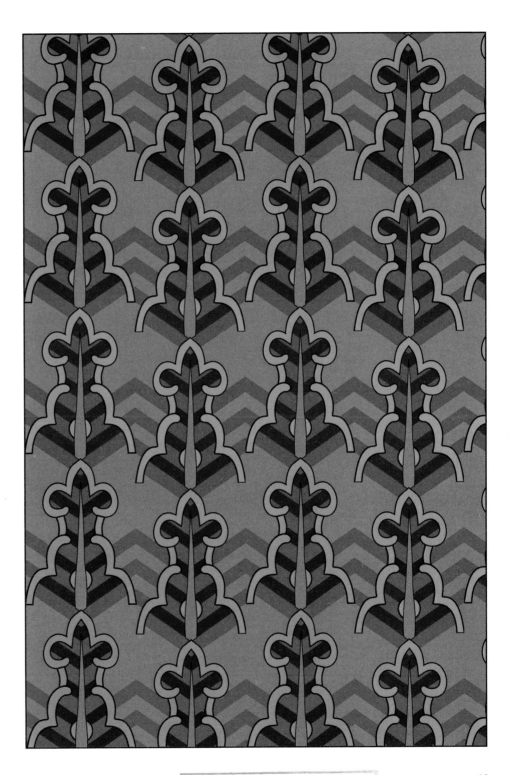

63

One-third drop repeat

Indian woodblock
print, 19th century

Quarter drop repeat

Art Deco design,
French, 1930s

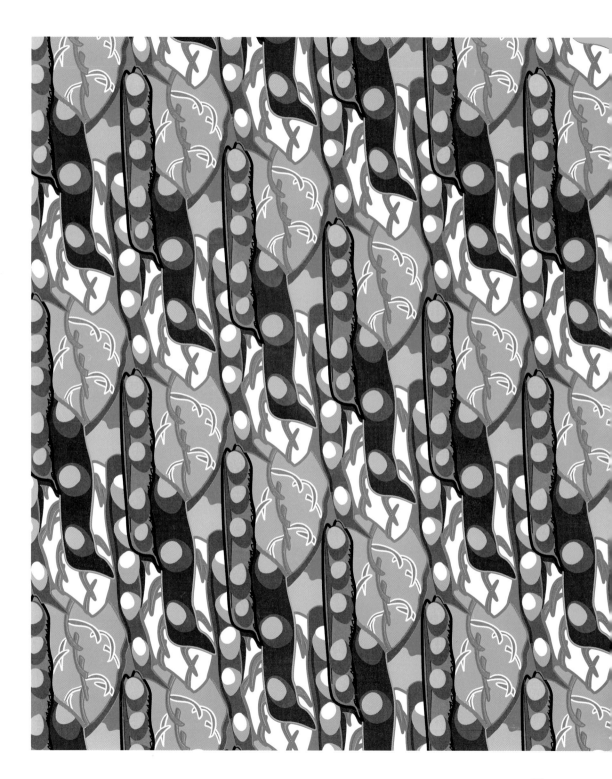

DROP REPEATS

Half drop pillar repeat

Right:
Medieval ornamental
design, based on
English crockets,
11th to 14th century
Below right:
Woodblocked textile
design, French,
mid–19th century

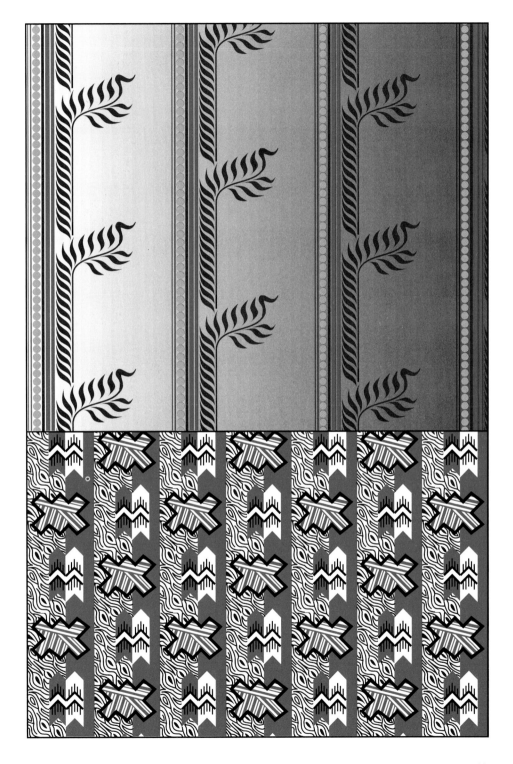

Open half drop repeat

FRENCH TEXTILE DESIGNS:

Right:

1825–50

Far right:

1800

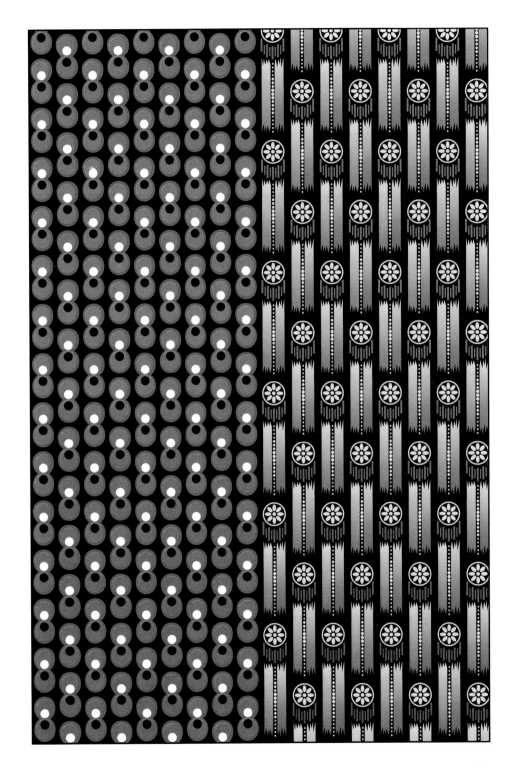

DROP REPEATS

Half drop repeat with
horizontal mirror, pillar
arrangement

Modernist pattern
wallpaper, 1934

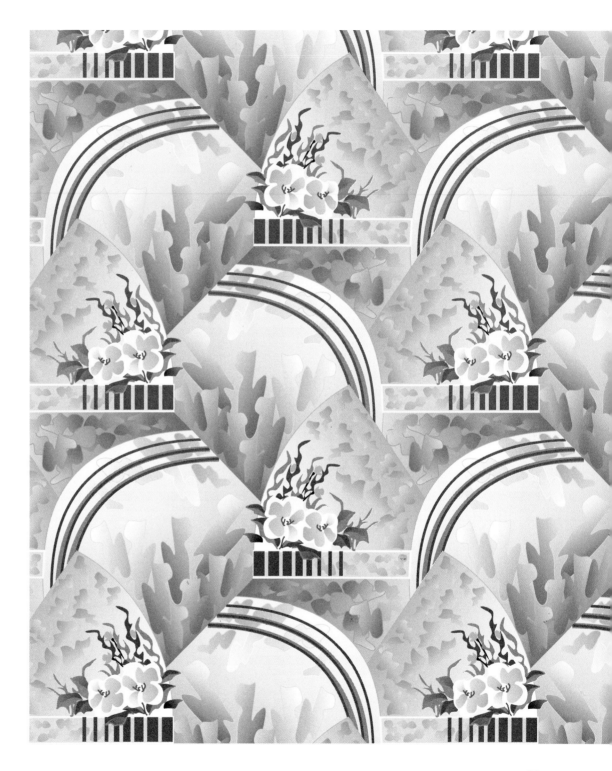

DROP REPEATS

Half drop repeat with
vertical mirror, pillar
arrangement

Paisley roller-printed textile, mid-19th century

DROP REPEATS

Half drop repeat with
rotation, pillar
arrangement

Warp ikat, Turkestan,
19th century

DROP REPEATS

Half drop repeat with
horizontal mirror,
stripe arrangement

English wallpaper
design, 1906

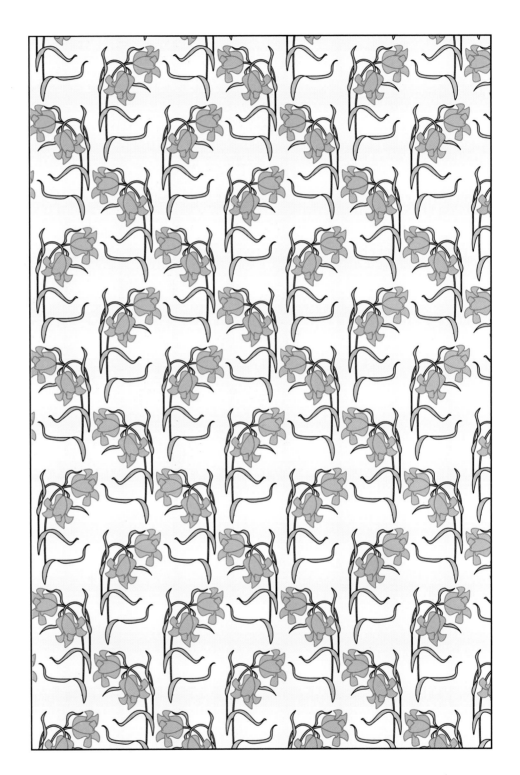

DROP REPEATS

Half drop repeat with
vertical mirror, stripe
arrangement

Anatolian kilim,
19th century

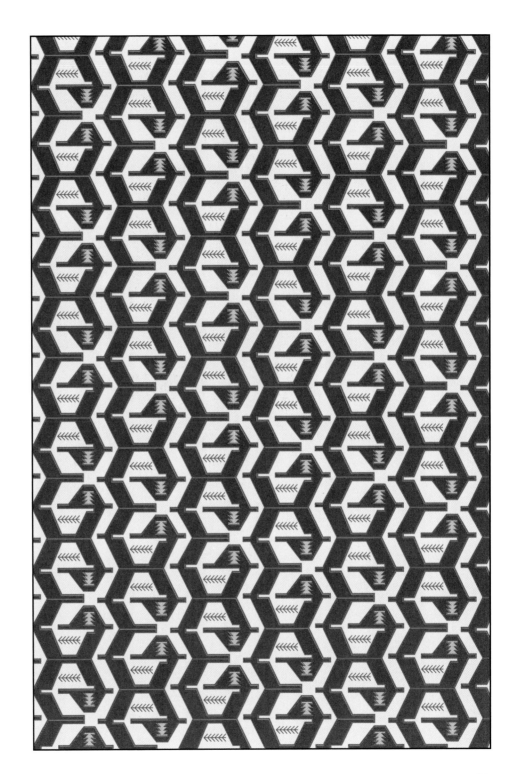

DROP REPEATS

Half drop repeat with
rotation, stripe
arrangement

Japanese kimono
pattern, 17th to 18th
century

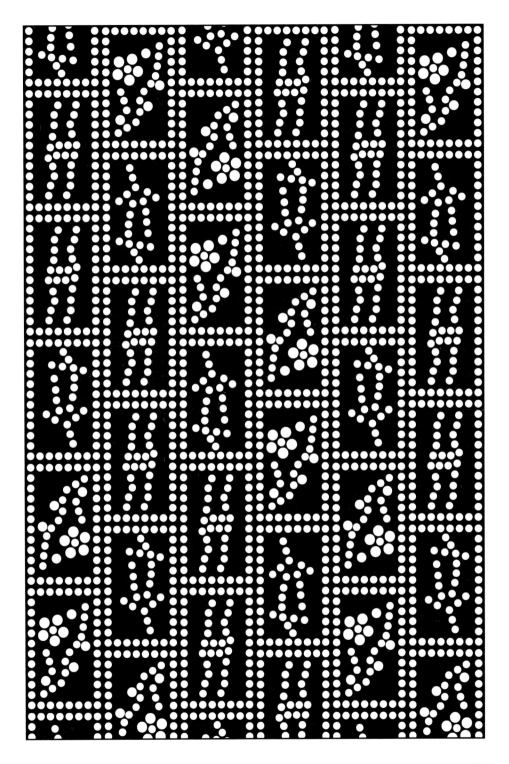

Chapter Three **BRICK REPEATS**

The brick repeat is similar to the half drop repeat, in that one rotated through 90 degrees produces the other. The main difference is that the brick repeat forms a horizontal emphasis, while the half drop results in a vertical one. It can also affect two-dimensional pattern by creating a diagonal movement, which can be emphasized or subdued by controlled application of colour and tone, which are used to link visually particular elements in the repeated design (page 89).

The most common variation is the striped horizontal mirror (page 105); in this case the curved line of the Paisley motif creates directional changes as the eye moves over the pattern. If the grid structure is used as an element within a design, it creates a more stable and solid pattern when repeated.

BRICK REPEATS

BRICK REPEATS:

(a) Brick repeat

(b) One-third brick

(c) Quarter brick
Spacing applied to (a)
produces (d) Horizontal
stripe, and (e) Open

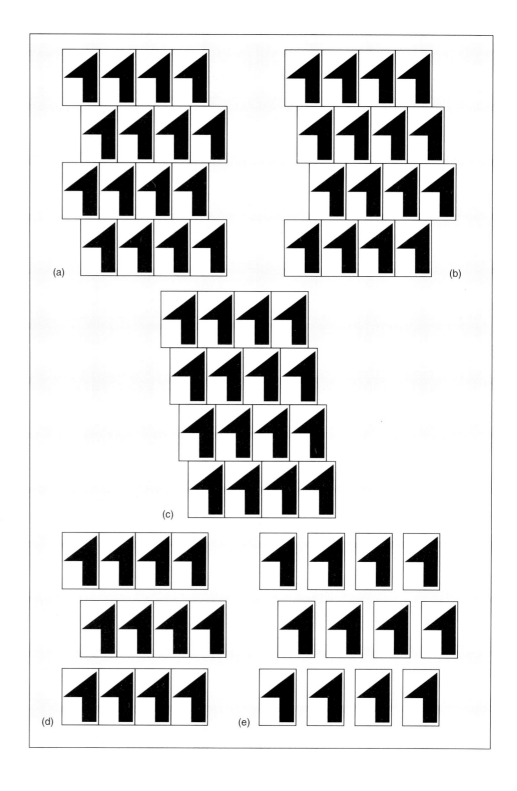

BRICK REPEAT VARIANTS:

Top row:

Horizontal mirror

Centre row:

Vertical mirror

Bottom row:

Rotation

(a) to (c) are pillar arrangements,

(d) to (f) are striped.

They can be used in any of the repeat formats shown on the page opposite

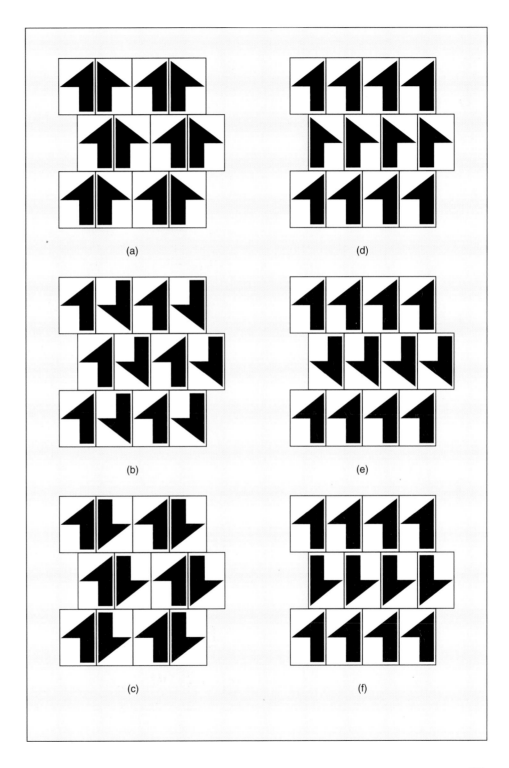

(a)

(b)

(c)

(d)

(e)

(f)

Brick repeat

Dutch textile design,
early 16th century

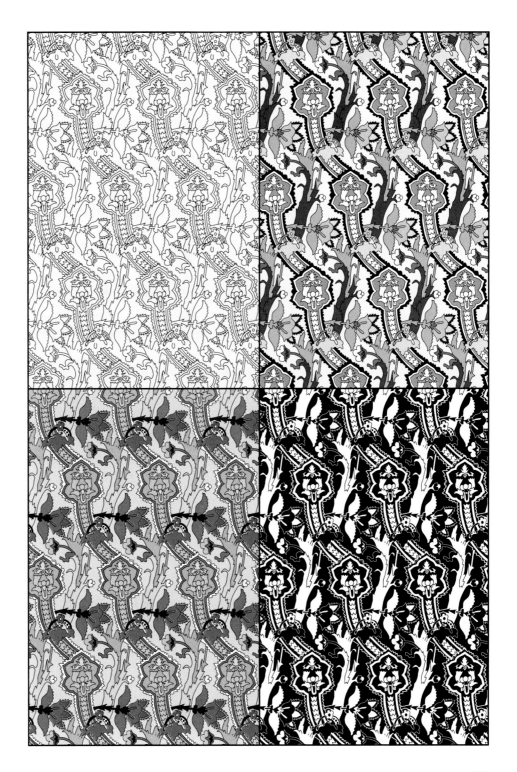

One-third brick repeat

French Art Deco
design, 1925

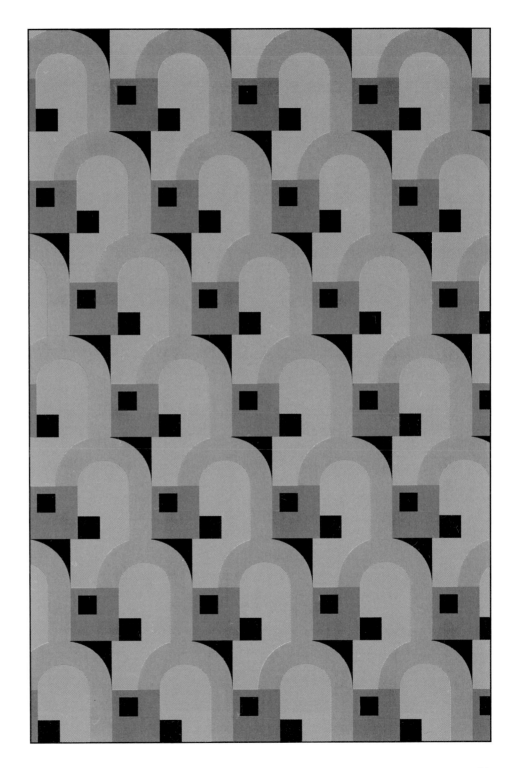

BRICK REPEATS

Quarter brick repeat

Pattern from a Peruvian
woven tunic, 13th to
14th century

BRICK REPEATS

Horizontal stripe brick
repeat

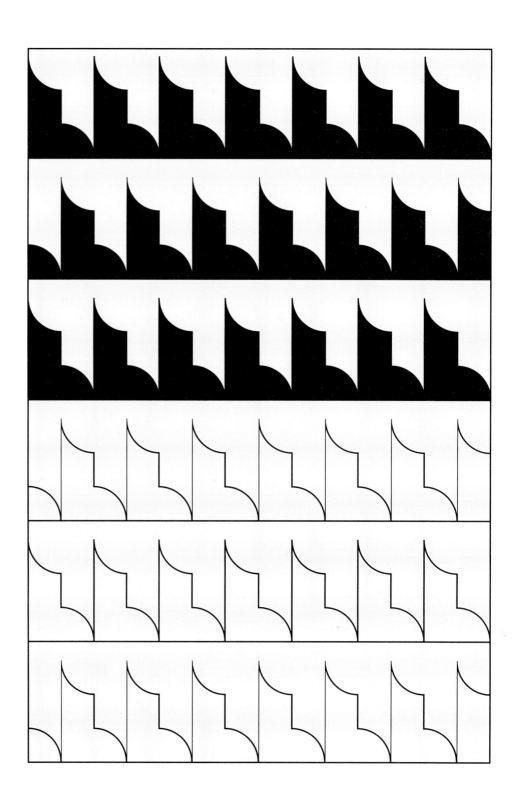

Russian Constructivist
design, late 1920s

BRICK REPEATS

Open brick repeat

Right:
Venetian book cover
showing Persian
influence, late 13th
century
Far right:
Background pattern
from a Persian
illuminated manuscript,
19th century
Below right:
British textile design,
1990

BRICK REPEATS

Brick repeat with
horizontal mirror,
pillar arrangement

American
contemporary Art Deco
design, 1989

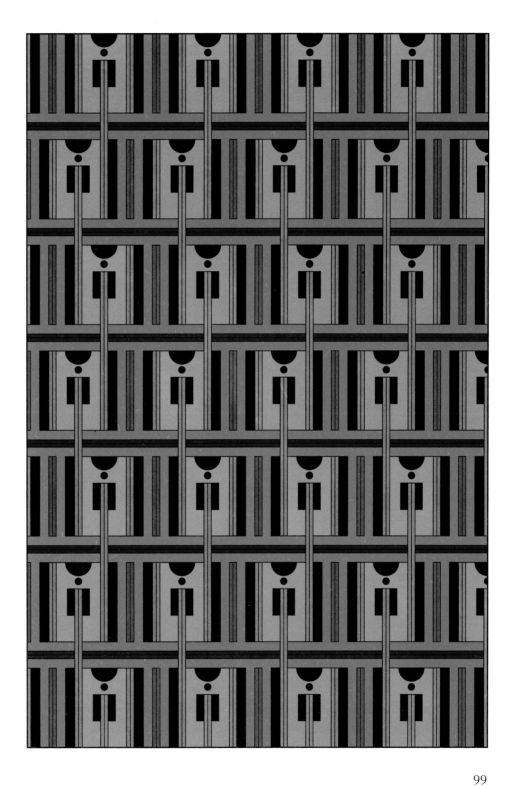

BRICK REPEATS

Brick repeat with
vertical mirror, pillar
arrangement

Right:
Filling pattern, French
shawl design, late 18th
century

Below right:
Geometric pattern from
North American Indian
basketwork, 19th
century

BRICK REPEATS

Brick repeat with
rotation, pillar
arrangement

Right:
Spiral pattern, Neolithic
vase decoration
Below right:
Detail from a
Turkoman prayer rug,
19th century

BRICK REPEATS

Brick with horizontal
mirror, stripe
arrangment

Filling pattern, British
Paisley shawl design,
mid–19th century

BRICK REPEATS

Brick repeat with
vertical mirror, stripe
arrangement

Russian Constructivist
design, late 1920s

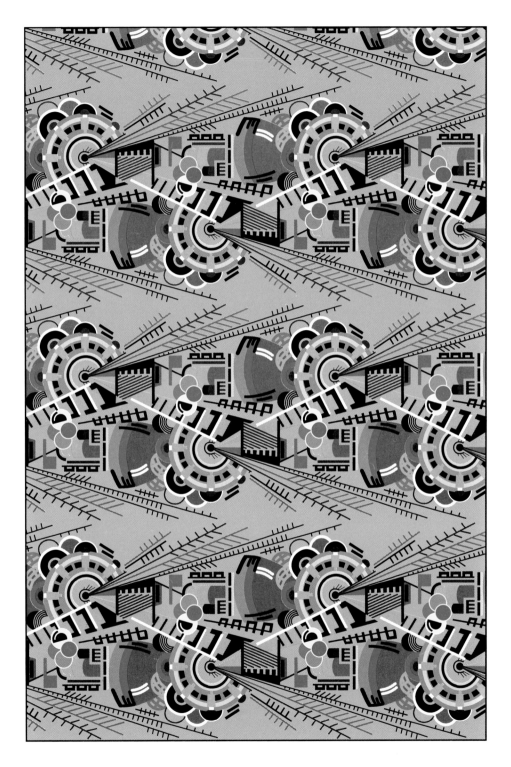

Brick repeat with
rotation, stripe
arrangement

Chinese textile design,
14th century

Chapter Four

IRREGULAR REPEATS

Irregular repeats, also known as step or sliding repeats, are based on the same principles as the drop and brick repeats. The difference lies in the fact that the consecutive units are not always moved through a fraction of the unit. Both types of repeat may be combined (as in the bottom example opposite, and page 117), and the drop is not always continued in a regular sequence. Changes in direction (page 113) and orientation (page 115) may be applied.

The examples shown here are only a small, representative selection from the many arrangements that can be created. Zig-zag formations and irregular systems give a sense of the irrational and create a more unpredictable effect. These stepped or sliding units can make a considerable difference to the size or emphasis of the repeats.

(a) Irregular step repeat

(b) Quarter drop repeat with horizontal mirror and reversed drop

(c) Combination of an irregular drop and irregular brick

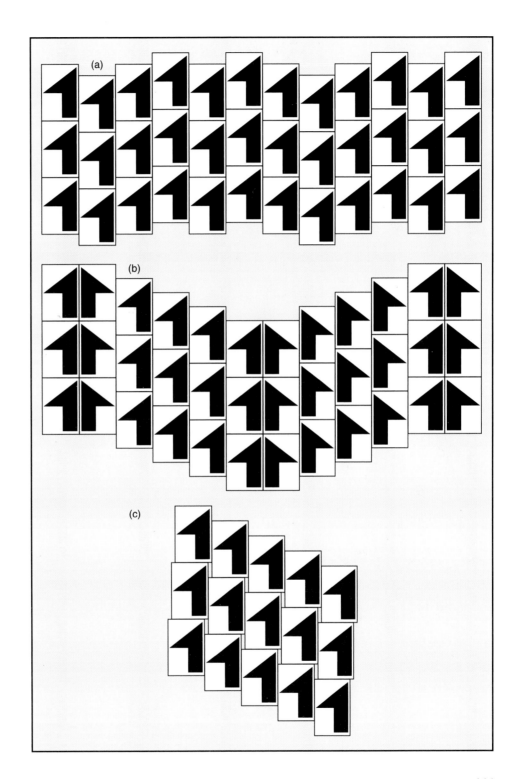

Irregular step repeat

Zig–zag pattern
demonstrating a
method commonly
used during the Middle
Ages for the decoration
of pillars

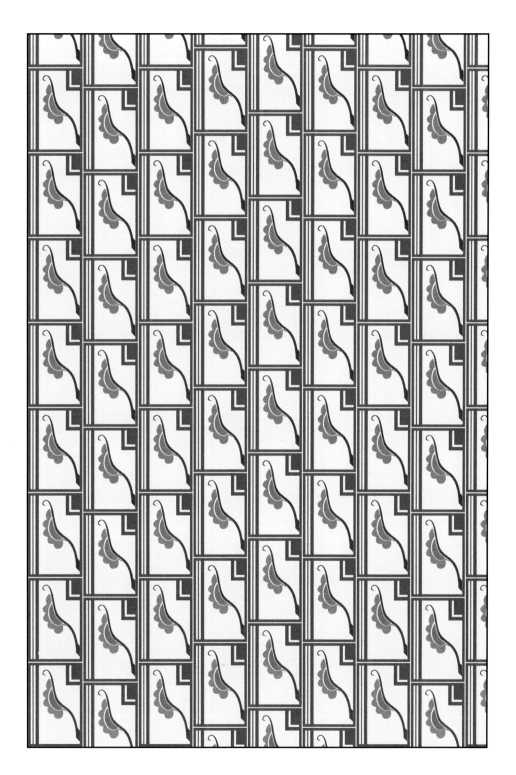

IRREGULAR REPEATS

Quarter drop repeat
with mirror and
reversed drop

Ikat weaving,
Turkestan, 19th
century

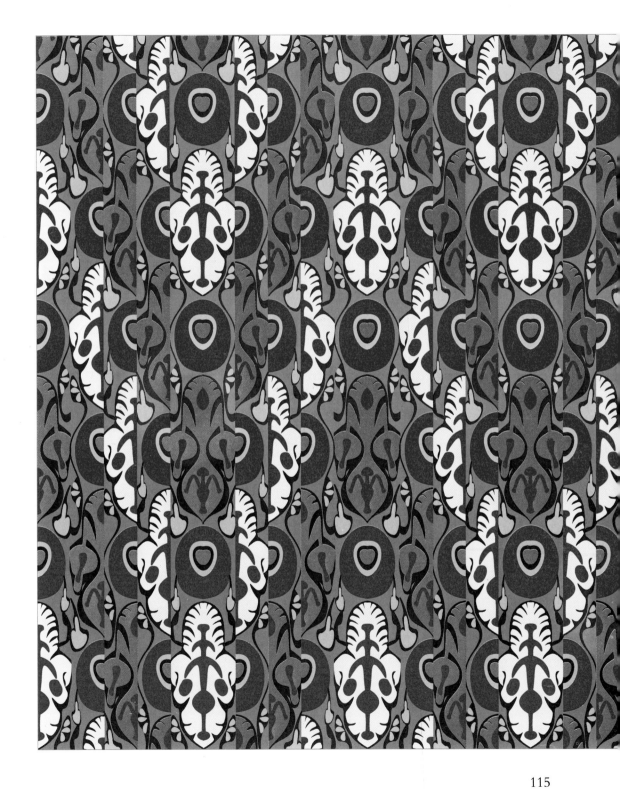

IRREGULAR REPEATS

A combination of
irregular drop and brick
repeats

Optical pattern, 1970s

Chapter Five　**COMPOSITE REPEATS**

A composite repeat is created from three or more design units, using rotation or mirroring techniques. The composite unit can then be repeated using any of the repeat systems. The example on page 121 shows a symmetrical repeat used extensively in textiles, tiles and many other areas of surface decoration. The hexagonal units are most commonly found in Islamic art (see page 131, below).

(a) Four-way mirror

(b) Alternating four-way mirror

(c) Rotated vertical mirror

(d) 90-degree rotation

(e) 120-degree rotation

(f) 60-degree rotation

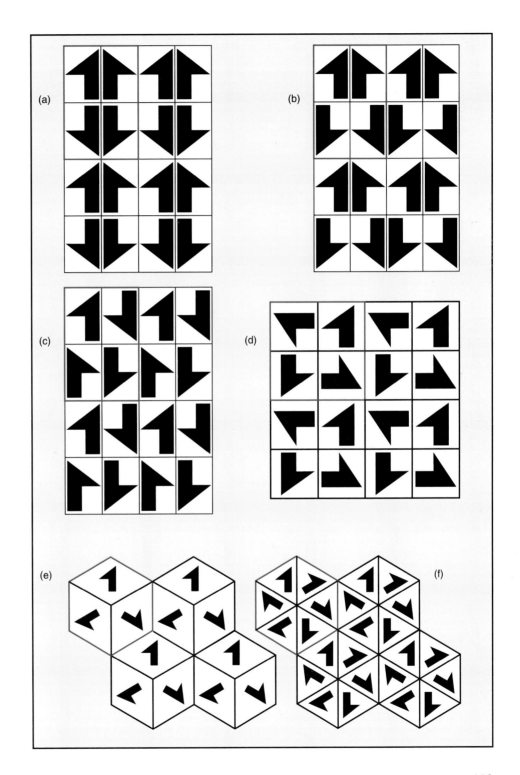

Four-way mirror repeat

Arts and Crafts
movement ceiling paper
design, late 19th
century

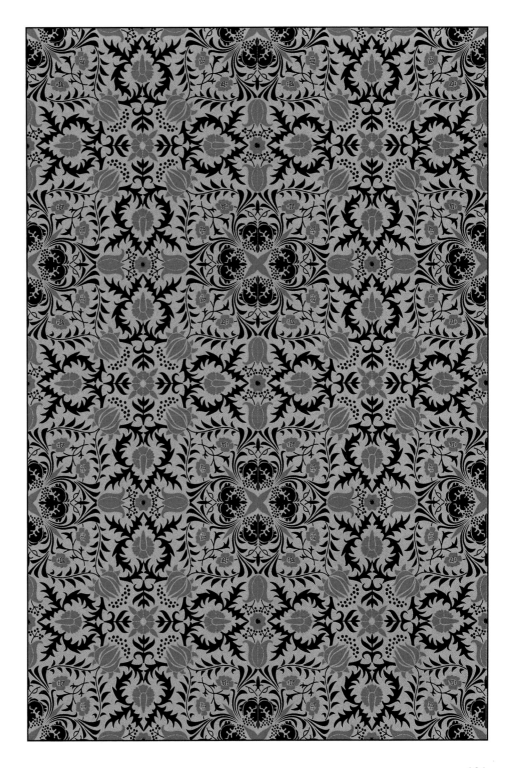

Alternating four-way
mirror

Right:
Fan pattern, 18th–
century Japanese fukusa
(textile gift cover)
Below right:
Egyptian ceiling
pattern, 7th century BC

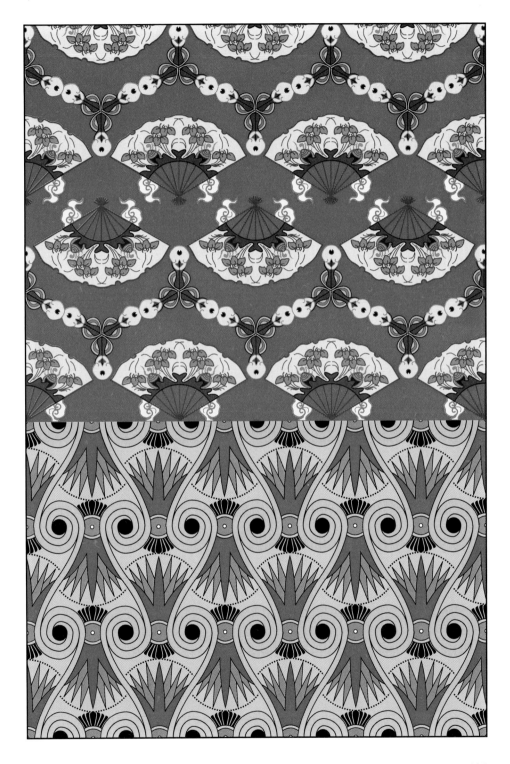

Composite repeat with
vertical mirror and
rotation

Woven shirt fabric,
Peruvian, 600–1000 AD

COMPOSITE REPEATS

Block repeat using
a composite unit
constructed by
90-degree rotations

Right:
Continuous pattern
from an illuminated
manuscript, British,
7th to 9th century
Below right:
Knot pattern, Pictish
stone cross carving,
8th century

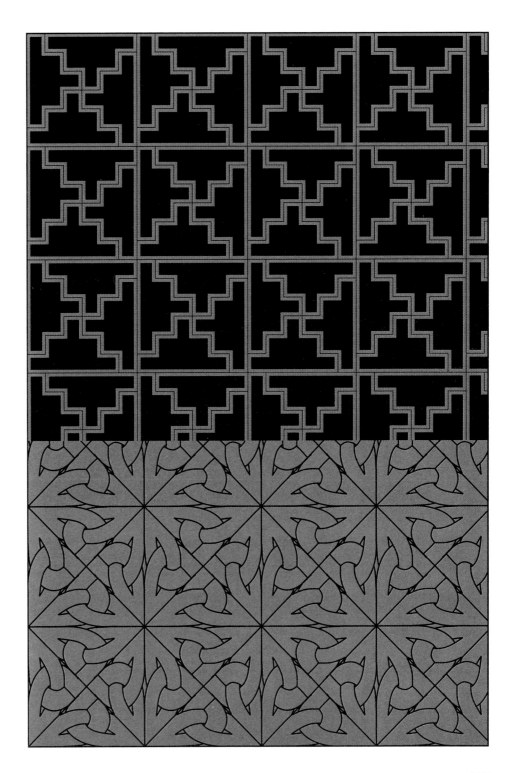

Composite repeat
constructed using
120-degree rotations

Textile design, late
1930s

COMPOSITE REPEATS

Composite repeat
constructed using
60-degree rotations

Right:
British textile design,
1951
Below right:
Iranian tile pattern,
5th to 11th century

Chapter Six   **SATEEN REPEATS**

Regular or irregular sateen or spot repeats lend the motifs a non-directional aspect. This creates the appearance of a free distribution of motifs and a flowing design concept, as the spots seem to be scattered at random. The advantages of this repeat system, especially over the drop repeats, are that:

i)   stripes are less likely to occur in the pattern organization;

ii) the design tends to be more effective because the fact that the main motifs can be placed in a variety of directions gives the pattern more movement;

iii) the actual repetition of the pattern is better concealed.

Sateen arrangements are often used as the basis for textile designs, and they are employed extensively in the home furnishings market. This repeat system is also frequently found in printed fashion fabrics designed for the garment industry, as it enables the lay-planning (the arrangement of the pattern pieces on the fabric) to be carried out in the most efficient and economical way.

The spot designs may appear to be simple and easy to create, but there are two main points that the designer should note:

i)   avoid the creation of 'repeat marks', unwanted gaps, holes or clusters, which might appear when the design is repeated;

ii) limit the scale of the motifs, as smaller masses tend to be more successful.

REGULAR SATEEN REPEATS
WITH COUNTS OF THREE:

Right:

Five-spot

Main picture, pattern;
inset, plan

Far right:

Pattern with some
motifs rotated; inset,
rotation plan

Below right:

Seven-spot treated
in the same manner

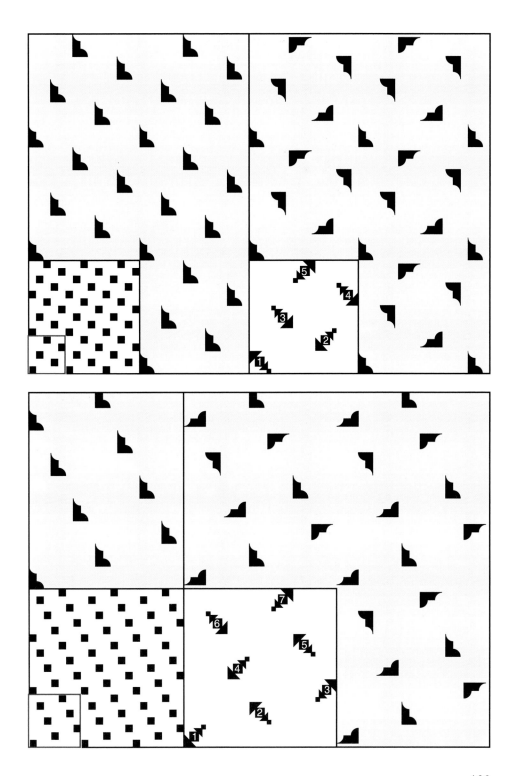

SATEEN REPEATS

Art Nouveau patterns
based on a regular
five-spot sateen, 1900

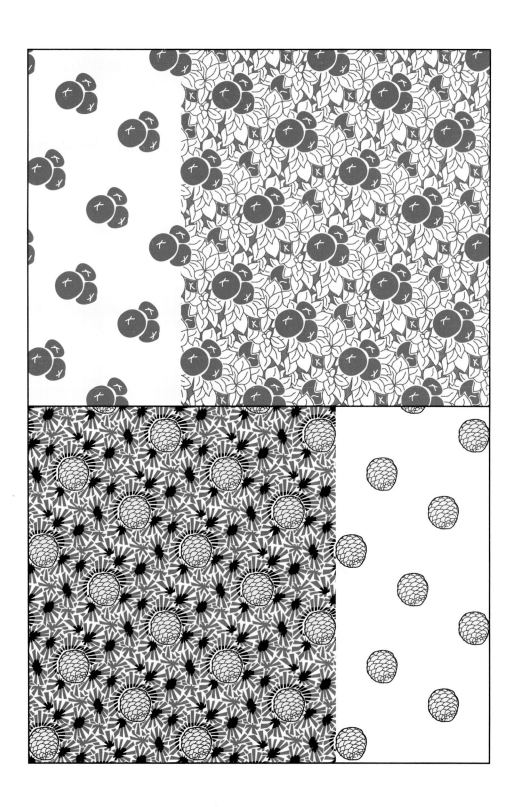

Pattern based on
a regular seven-spot
sateen, with mirrored
motifs. French textile
design, 1800

SATEEN REPEATS

IRREGULAR SATEEN REPEATS
WITH INSET PATTERN AND
ROTATION PLANS:
Right:
Six-spot
Below right:
Eight-spot

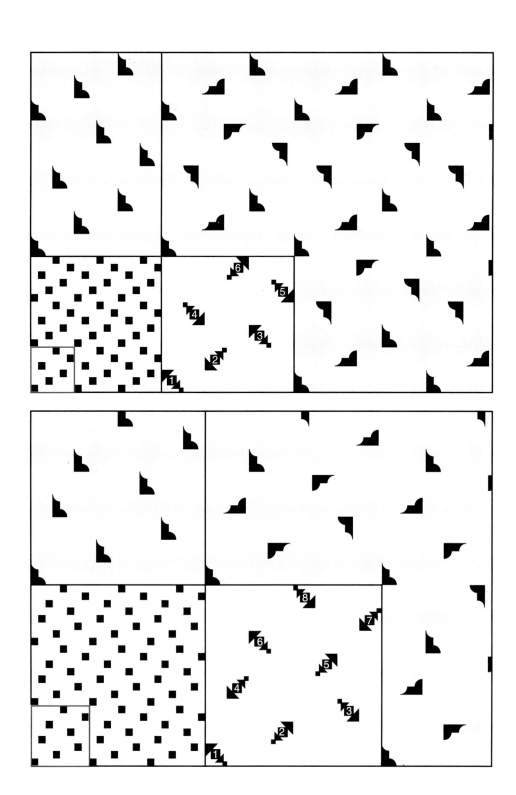

Pattern based on an
irregular six-spot sateen,
1990s

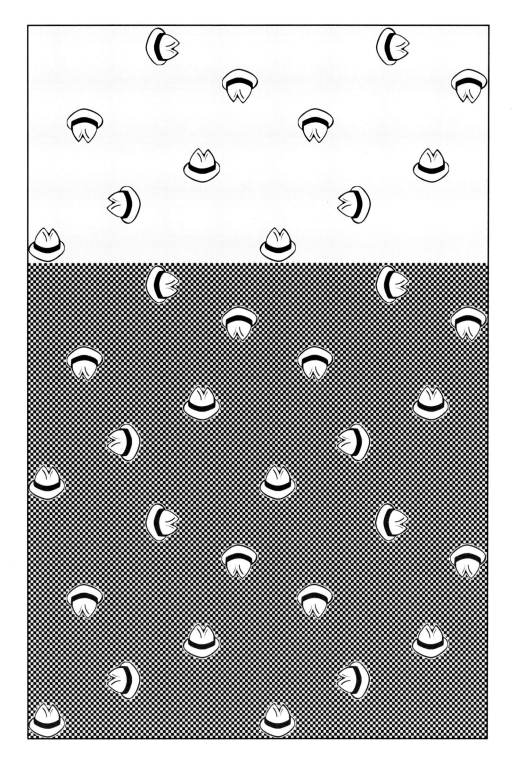

Pattern based on an
irregular eight-spot
sateen, with 90-degree
rotations. French
printed textile design,
1800

Chapter Seven

BANDS AND BORDERS

For the designer, the most interesting and exciting aspect of borders (bands) and panels is the vast range of design solutions that can be achieved when consideration needs to be given to edges, centres and corners. Borders and panels have been used extensively in many cultures. Magnificent examples of what may be described as 'enclosed ornament' can be discovered in numerous fields of art and design: Japanese kimonos, wrought ironwork, Caucasian village rugs, decorative plasterwork and Meissen porcelain.

The boundaries of discontinuous or panel ornament are arbitrary and can be considered in relation to the following shapes: the square and other regular polygons, the circle, oblong, ellipse, lozenge and triangle. Within these shapes the potential for decorative detail is infinitely varied, repeated patterns and single units being used independently and in conjunction to create the desired effects.

The ability to deal with issues of proportion and variations in scale is the essence of good design in this area of study. Contemporary trends have witnessed their use in both the fashion and interior design markets. Borders are also used to create illusions of length, width, height and depth when applied to surface areas.

BANDS AND BORDERS

BAND PATTERNS:

(a) Block

(b) Block – vertical mirror

(c) Block – horizontal mirror

(d) Block – rotation

(e) Brick – vertical mirror

(f) Block – four-way mirror

(g) Block – alternating mirror

(h) Block – 180-degree rotation pillar

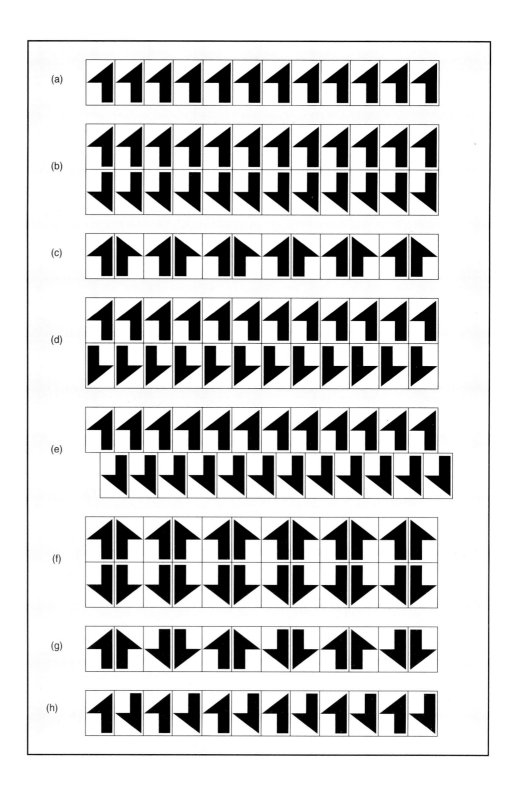

Band (a):
Egyptian woven band,
7th to 8th century,
and English stencilled
fabric design, early
20th century

Band (b):
American block-printed
fabric, early 19th
century

(a)

(b)

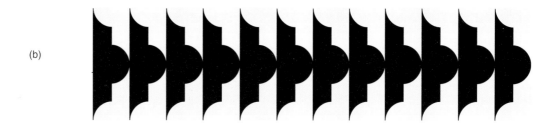

BANDS AND BORDERS

Band (c):
Chancay embroidered
panel, Peruvian,
11th to 15th century,
and cresting on
carved wooden choir stall,
English, 15th century
Band (d):
Attic painted vase,
5th to 6th century

(c)

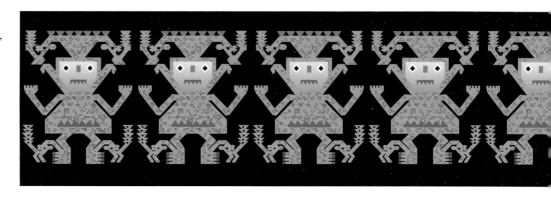

(d)

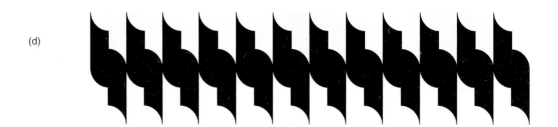

Band (e):
Egypto-Roman woven
band, 3rd to 5th
century

Band (f):
Classical Greek fret
pattern, and North
American Indian loom–
woven beadwork, 19th
century

(e)

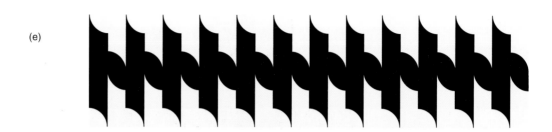

(f)

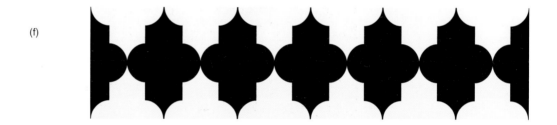

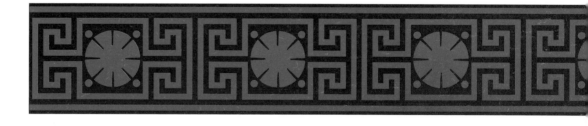

Band (g):
Enamelled earthenware
tile, Turkish, 17th
century
Band (h):
Two French Art Deco
designs, 1930, and
Egyptian tapestry-
woven band, 3rd to 4th
century

(g)

(h)

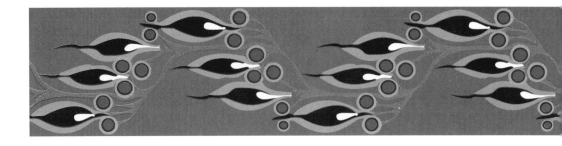

Right:
Border composed of
units of the same
orientation, with
repeating pattern on
central area
Far right:
Arts and Crafts textile,
late 19th century
Below right:
Border employing
90-degree rotation of
units at the corner, with
consecutive borders and
a central design
Below, far right:
Persian rug,
19th century

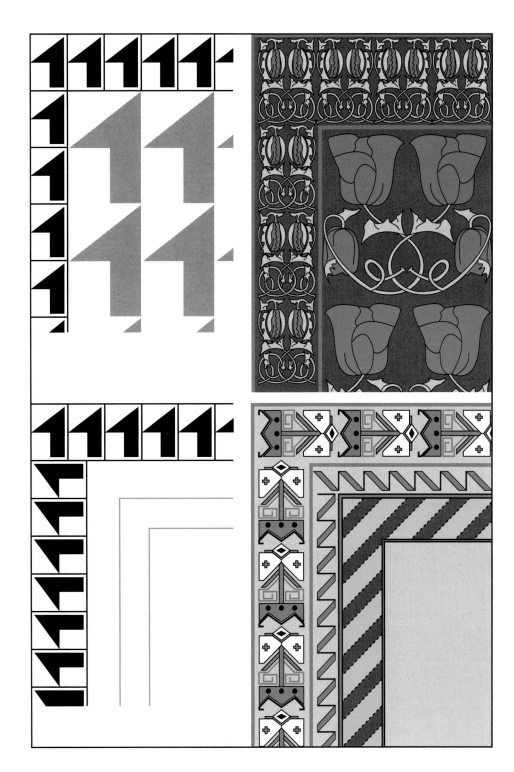

Right:
Border with 90-degree rotation and second unit at the corner, surrounding a single design

Far right:
French glass painting, 13th century

Below right:
Mitred corner on border surrounding a rotated design

Below, far right:
Greek ceiling painting, 5th century BC

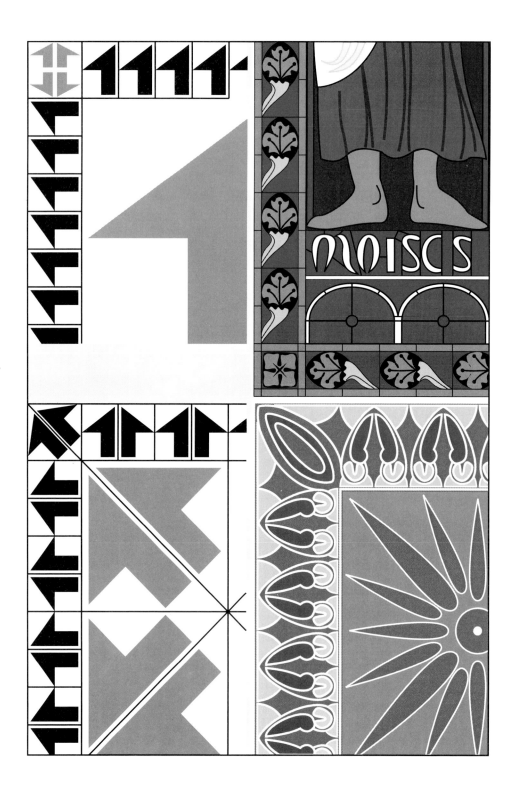

Chapter Eight

COMPOSITE OVERLAYS

Composite overlays are created when one repeat system is overlaid (superimposed) by another. Various combinations of structure and design can be used. The interaction of these structures produces unexpected and exciting pattern variations. The simplest scheme is to overprint a design with a copy of that same design which has been offset horizontally and/or vertically (see pages 148-150).

The creation of a third colour can be achieved by the overprinting of the two original colours in certain areas (page 151). The copy can also be mirrored or rotated (pages 151 above, 152 above). Alternatively, two different repeat structures and designs can be used (pages 152 below, to 154). However, if the scale of the repeats being superimposed differs, it is essential that they be proportionate (page 151 below).

COMPOSITE OVERLAYS

COMPOSITE OVERLAYS
FORMED BY OFFSETTING
A COPY OF THE REPEAT:
Right:
Block repeat moved
horizontally and
vertically
Below right:
90-degree rotation
repeat moved by half
the width and height
of the composite unit

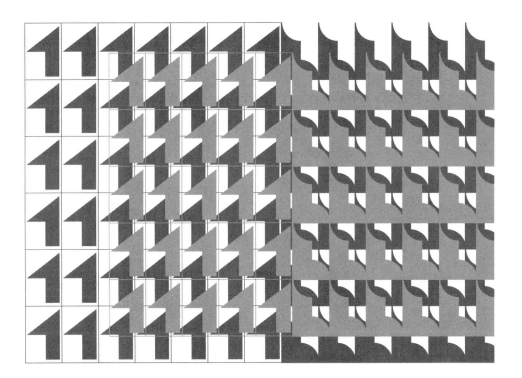

148

Block repeat overlay. The copy is offset both horizontally and vertically. American block-printed fabric, 1890

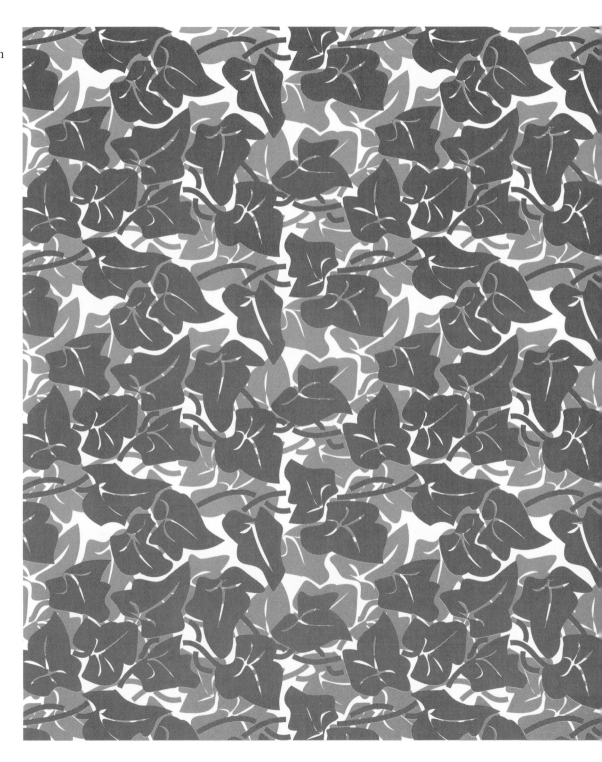

COMPOSITE OVERLAYS

OVERLAYS FORMED USING
ROTATIONAL REPEATS:
Right:
Watercolour, Dutch,
1930s
Below right:
Persian tiles,
11th century

Right:
Brick repeat overlaid by
a copy rotated through
180 degrees
Below right:
Block repeat overlaid
by a larger-scale brick
repeat

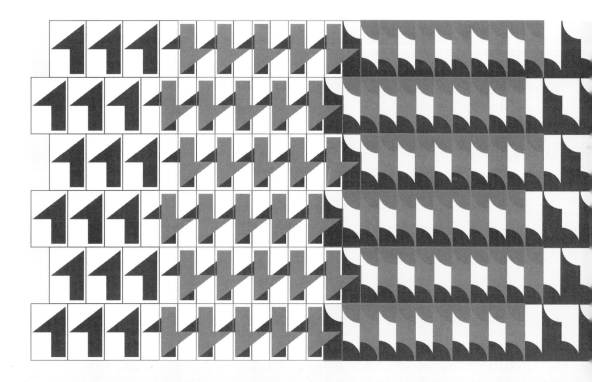

COMPOSITE OVERLAYS

Right:
Brick repeat overlaid
by a rotated copy.
Printed curtain fabric,
American, 1950s

Below right:
Block repeat with an
overlaid brick repeat.
Printed textile, British,
1980s

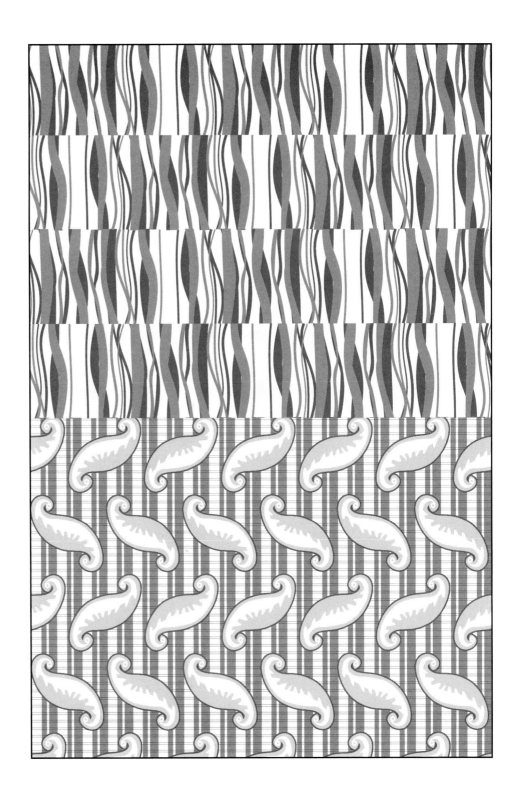

Block diaper mirror repeat overlaid by a half drop repeat. French Art Nouveau design, 1900

COMPOSITE OVERLAYS

Right:
Open brick repeat and
smaller-scale brick
repeat. Art Nouveau,
French, 1900
Below right:
Small-scale brick repeat
and open brick repeat
with rotation. Japanese
Samurai pattern from a
fubako (painted box)

Chapter Nine

COUNTERCHANGED REPEATS

The term counterchange (negative – positive) is applied to designs in which the shape and/or colour change positions. It is essential for the designer to consider not only the positive forms, and how they relate to each other, but the negative areas that remain. This system is an effective way of extending the repeat size, creating optical effects and changing the emphasis of a motif, whilst maintaining forms of exactly the same proportion.

Counterchange with
basic repeats

BLOCKS:

(a) Pillar

(b) Stripe

(c) Diaper

DROPS:

(d) Pillar

(e) Stripe

(f) Diagonal

BRICKS:

(g) Pillar

(h) Stripe

(i) Diagonal

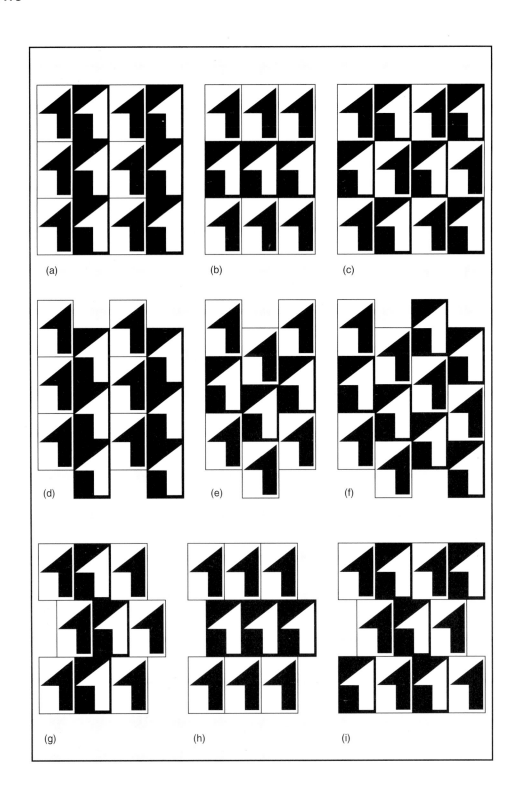

(a)   (b)   (c)

(d)   (e)   (f)

(g)   (h)   (i)

BLOCK REPEATS:

Right:

Pillar counterchange.

Indian printed chintz,

19th century

Below right:

Striped counterchange.

Egyptian pattern, 18th

to 20th Dynasty

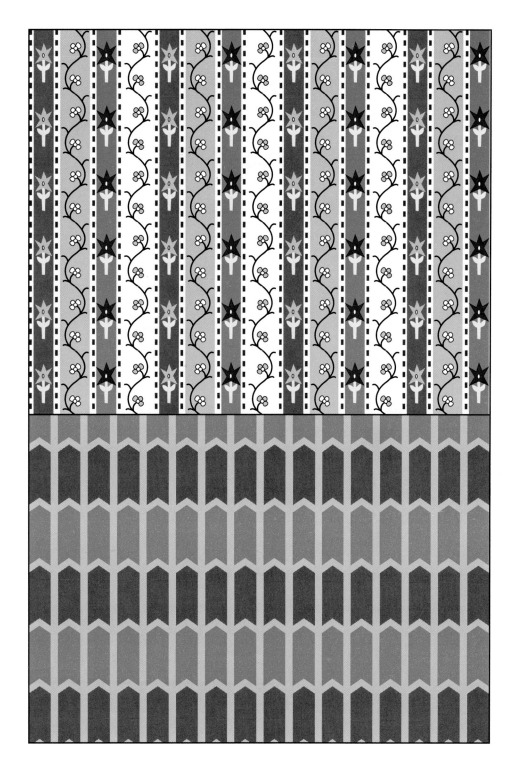

COUNTERCHANGED REPEATS

Block repeat with
diaper counterchange.
Wallpaper design, 1970s

158

Half drop repeat with
pillar counterchange.
Design for leggings,
1991

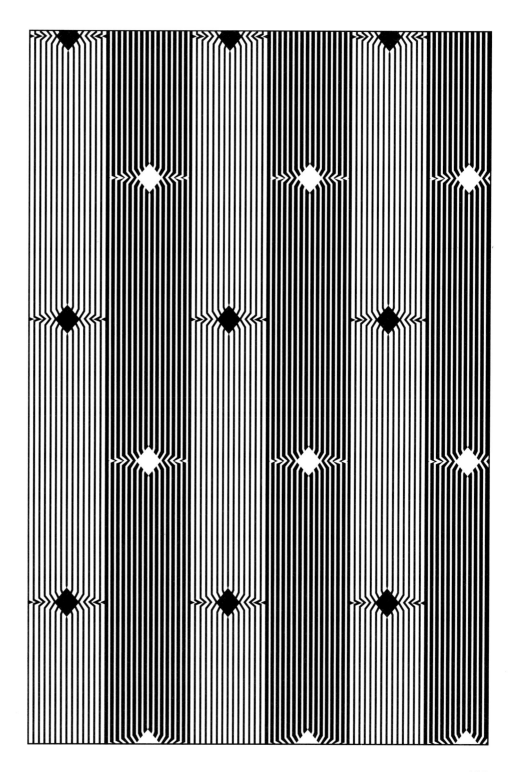

COUNTERCHANGED REPEATS

HALF DROP REPEATS:

Right:

Striped counterchange.
Byzantine floor mosaic

Below right:

Diagonal
counterchange. French
Art Deco design, 1920s

Brick repeat with
striped horizontal
mirror and pillar
counterchange. Persian
rug, 19th century

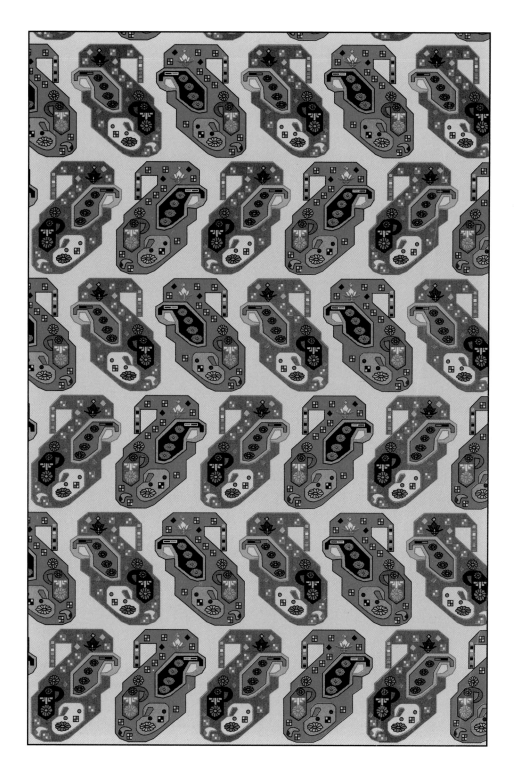

COUNTERCHANGED REPEATS

BRICK REPEATS:

Right:

With striped counterchange. Dutch watercolour, 1950s

Below right:

With diagonal counterchange. Caucasian rug, early 19th century

162

Chapter Ten

WOODBLOCK REPEATS

The woodblock construction evolves from two main network structures: parquet and diapers. Parquet wooden flooring, consisting of pieces of the same or different shapes, can be arranged to create a wide variety of pattern organizations. Diapers are generally seen in panels and on wall surfaces, but this method of repeat has great potential for many other areas of surface design.

Designs are often geometric, and linear forms are accentuated by the 90-degree turn (see page 169). This can also be an interesting arrangement for small motifs, and it helps to enlarge the repeat size (page 167).

WOODBLOCK REPEATS

(a) Woodblock repeat
(b) Counterchanged
woodblock repeat,
diagonal arrangement.
The coloured lines
show the larger repeat
units

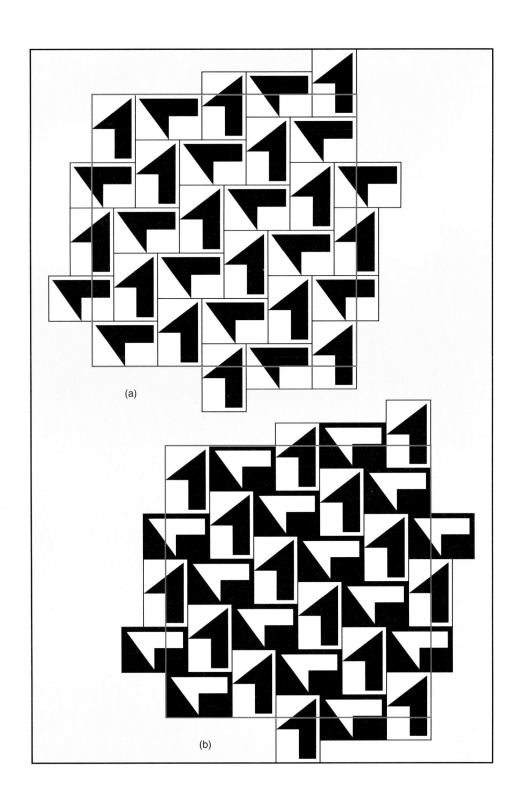

(a)

(b)

Counterchanged
woodblock repeat,
stepped arrangement.
The coloured line
shows the larger repeat
unit

Woodblock repeat

European brocade designs, late 16th century

WOODBLOCK REPEATS

COUNTERCHANGED
WOODBLOCK REPEATS:
Right:
Diagonal
Below right:
Stepped

COUNTERCHANGED
WOODBLOCK REPEATS:
Right:
Diagonal
Below right:
Stepped. Ceiling
paintings from ancient
Egyptian tombs

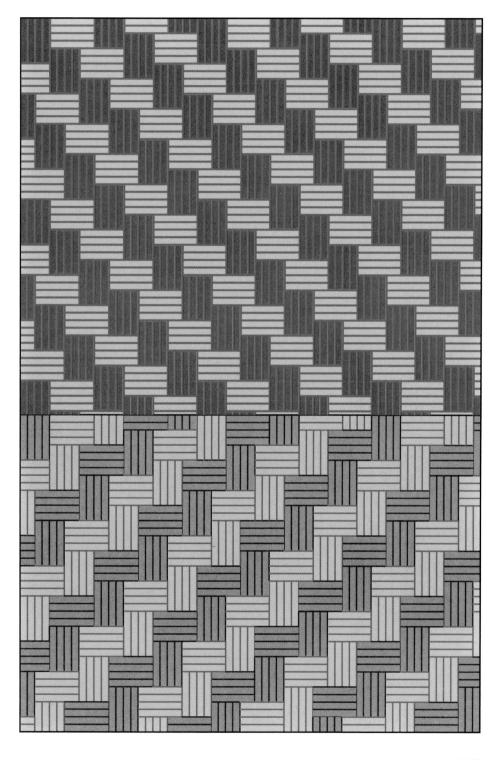

Chapter Eleven

SCALE AND GRADATION

Gradation, like a mathematical equation, is a strict discipline; it demands gradual change in an orderly way. It generates optical illusions, and creates a sense of progression that leads to an explosive focal point or series of focal points (page 176).

Concepts of gradation are an everyday experience. Objects that are in close proximity appear larger than those at a distance, which are infinitely smaller. Imagine viewing from a low angle a tall building with a facade of regular window patterns; the gradual change in size of the windows suggests a law of gradation.

Unit forms can be used in gradation within a repetition structure. Most visual and relational elements can be used singly or combined in gradation, to achieve various effects. The introduction of scale and movement produces radiation, which can be explained as the 'special effects' of repetition. Radiation can have the effect of optical vibration, which is useful when a powerful, eye-catching design is required. It is also a phenomenon found in nature; a good example is a flower in bloom, which creates radiation patterns through the arrangement of its petals. Unit forms may be graduated in shape, size, colour, texture, direction, position and space.

Scaled units

Pattern formed using
different sizes of the
same unit

Pattern formed by rows
of motifs in three
different sizes. Persian
rug, 19th century

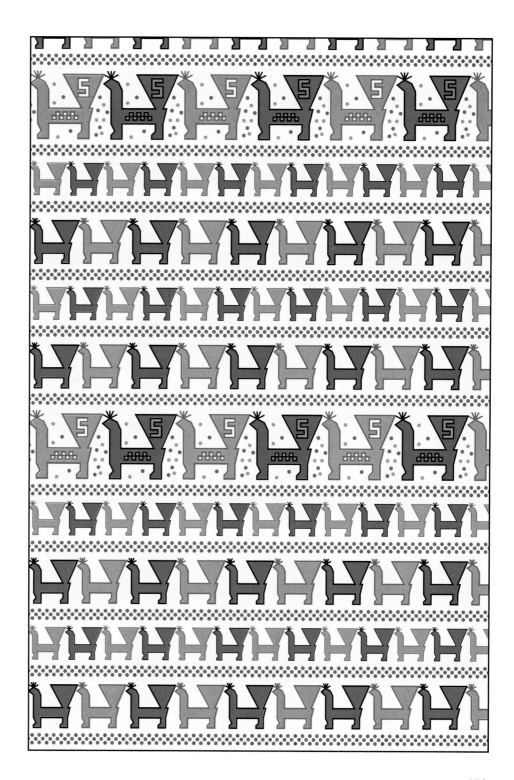

Right:
Byzantine marble
pavement. The same
triangular motif is
changed in scale, and
the striped effect is
achieved by the use
of counterchange
Below right:
Optical pattern using
gradation

Right:
Design using gradation
of the central squares of
the units. Paper carrier
bag, 1970s

Optical pattern using
rotation and gradation
on both the horizontal
and vertical axes

176

Ancient Egyptian
papyrus pattern using
gradation

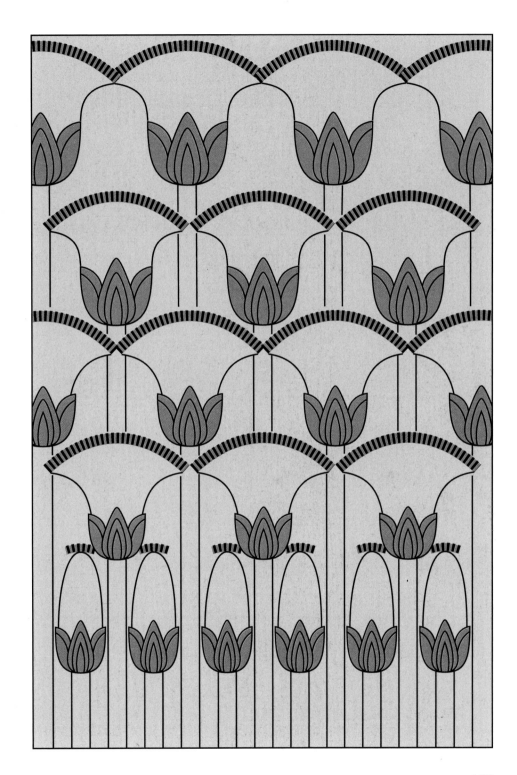

Chapter Twelve

TEXTURE

Texture has unique qualities that must be considered as an integral part of the creative process. The use of textural effects can create unexpected movement and patterns (page 184). When used in conjunction with the unit forms and combined with the repeat systems, texture can help to defuse and soften the basic shapes. It can also produce shadow or highlighting effects, giving the resulting patterns a three-dimensional quality and additional surface interest.

Texture refers to the surface characteristics of a shape. Every shape has a surface, the qualities of which may be described as smooth or rough, plain or decorated, matt or glossy, soft or hard. Nature contains a wealth of textures. Each kind of stone, wood or fabric possesses a distinct texture which can be exploited by the architect, designer or artist. The surfaces of the materials can also be finished in any number of ways to introduce greater diversity and extend the tonal range.

Texture can be classified into two important categories: visual and tactile. The appropriate texture adds richness and enhances the design concept.

Various types of texture
applied to a repeat unit

TEXTURE

Diaper arrangement of
textures used in block
repeats

Right:
Half drop repeat with
horizontal mirror
Below right:
Block repeat with four-
way mirror

Wallpaper design, 1970

Half drop repeat with
textures applied to the
motifs. 1950s furnishing
textile

Wallpaper design,
early 1950s

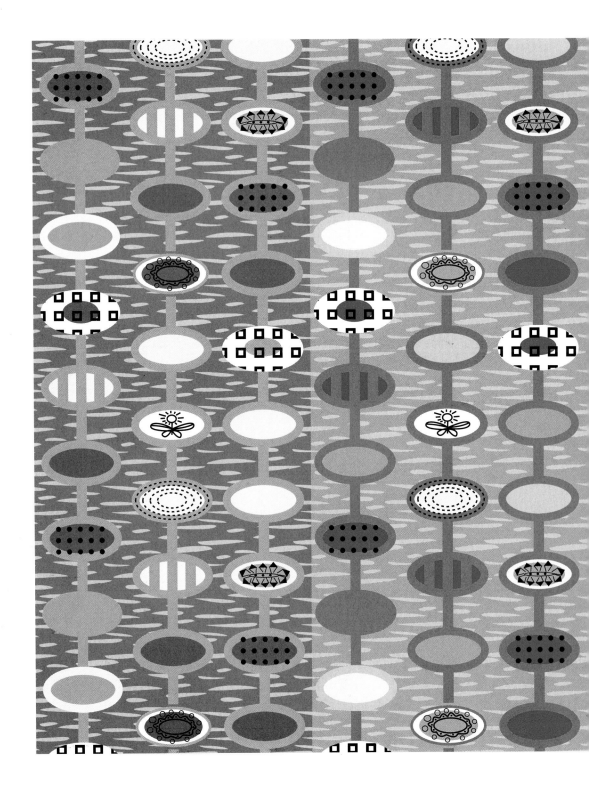

Design using various
textures applied to the
same motif. German
printed textile, 1930

Chapter Thirteen

ILLUSIONS: OPTICAL PHENOMENA

Psychologists, physicists, artists and writers have put forward many theories concerning the nature of illusion, but no single explanation answers all the questions convincingly. Certainly, illusions should not be dismissed as the trivial effects of certain patterns, but recognized as tools for investigating the basic processes involved in seeing the world. The following pages give an initial insight into yet another area in which repeat patterns can be fruitfully explored.

The first example (page 187) gives a simplified analytical treatment of the moiré effect; the second (page 188) illustrates the part angles can play in the creation of optical illusions, and the third (page 189) demonstrates how our eyes play tricks on us when we try to distinguish an image from its background. The juxtaposition of light and dark contrasts (page 190) creates illusions of tonal variation and feelings of different spatial placing.

The images that follow are just a foretaste of the countless possibilities that exist in this fascinating area of research.

The moiré effect occurs when two or more patterns made up of geometric units are overlapped. It is most pronounced when the spacing between the repeated elements in each pattern is nearly equal, and the angle of intersection between the two patterns is small

Right:
Linear and circular elements

Centre right:
The elements combined

Below right:
The effect produced by changing the scale of one element

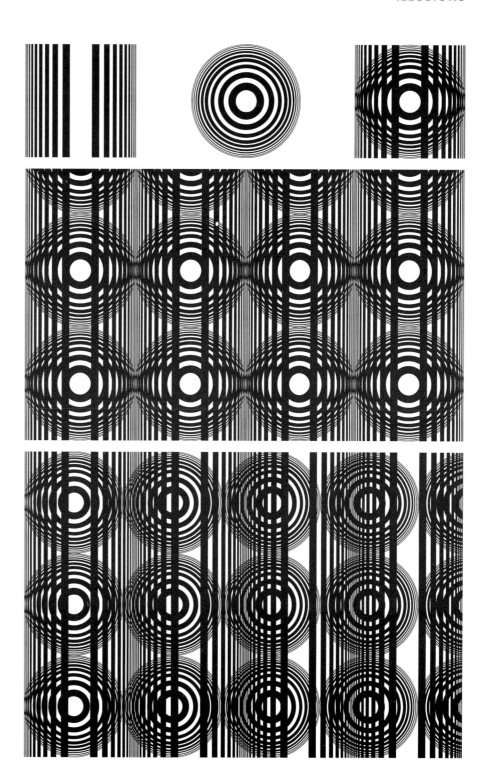

Angles play an
important part in many
illusions. In this pattern
the vertical lines are
visually distorted by the
use of angled lines
Far right, above:
Hering's illusion states
that two parallel lines
will appear to bend
outwards opposite the
point where the angled
lines converge
Far right, below:
According to Wundt's
illusion, when the point
of convergence lies
outside the parallel
lines, the lines appear to
diverge

Many optical illusions
relate to our capacity
to separate an object
from its general
environment. Various
factors, such as size,
shape, value and
closure, determine
which pieces of
information are
perceived as figure, and
which become the
subordinate ground.
Some figure/ground
images may be
experienced as
equivocal or reversible
relationships. Here,
a composite repeat is
formed by 120-degree
rotations of a pattern
element that has been
distorted into a
rhombus

ILLUSIONS

Colours, when juxtaposed, play tricks with the eye because the same hue appears to change by induction from differing backgrounds. This phenomenon, named 'simultaneous contrast' by the French chemist Michel-Eugène Chevreul, is demonstrated here by creating illusions of tonal variation of a single colour, red. The Bauhaus artist Johannes Itten was one of many who have explored types of colour contrast in their work

Peter Phillips M.Des. R.C.A, M.C.S.D

Peter Phillips graduated from the Royal College of Art in 1971, after specializing in printed textiles, and became a Member of the Chartered Society of Designers in 1978.

He established a design practice with Sue Newton-Mason, undertaking commissioned work and selling designs to leading manufacturers in the United Kingdom, Europe and America for the interior and fashion markets. He has exhibited design collections at international trade fairs and design exhibitions in Frankfurt, Amsterdam and London.

In 1979 he entered education as a senior lecturer on the BA (Hons) Textile Design course at Nottingham Polytechnic, and he now holds the position of Courses Director in the Department of Fashion and Textiles. He is currently researching and investigating computer systems that link C.A.D. and C.A.M. in the area of printed textiles.

Gillian Bunce

Gillian Bunce originally studied fine art and went on to make wall hangings and sculptures using textile materials. Her 'discovery' of the image manipulation capabilities of computer graphics resulted in the change from tactile to technological media.

She worked for three years as a computer graphics consultant at Leicester Polytechnic, working with industrial clients and design students on a wide range of computer graphics applications.

She is currently conducting research at Nottingham Polytechnic into the effects that developments in textile printing machinery and computer technology have had on the use of repeat structures in the design and production of printed textiles.

Bibliography

Albarn, K., J.M. Smith, S. Steele and D. Walker, *The Language of Pattern*, 1974

Allen, J., *The Designer's Guide to Japanese Patterns*, 1989; *The Designer's Guide to Samurai Patterns*, 1990

Audsley, W. and G., *Designs and Patterns from Historical Ornament*, 1968 (first published 1882)

Baglivo, J.A., and J.E. Graver, *Incidence and Symmetry in Design and Architecture*, 1983

Bain, I., *Celtic Knotwork*, 1986

Beauclair, R., *Art Nouveau Patterns and Designs*, 1988 (first published 1900)

Benedictus, E., *Art Deco Designs*, 1988 (first published 1926)

Biriukova, N., *West European Printed Textiles 16th – 18th Century*, 1973

Bourgoin, J., *Arabic Geometrical Pattern and Design*, 1973

Brédif, J., *Toiles de Jouy*, 1989

Cambridge Library of Ornamental Art, *Arabian Ornament*, 1991; *Japanese Ornament*, 1991; *Medieval Ornament*, 1991; *Renaissance Ornament*, 1991

Christie, A., *Pattern Design*, 1969

Critchlow, K., *Islamic Patterns*, 1976

Danby, M., *Grammar of Architectural Design*, 1963

Day, L.F., *The Anatomy of Pattern*, 1887

Dresser, C., *Studies in Design*, 1988 (first published 1876)

Dupont-Auberville, M., *Classic Textile Designs*, 1989 (first published 1877)

Durant, S., *Victorian Ornamental Design*, 1972

Edwards, E.B., *Pattern and Design with Dynamic Symmetry*, 1967

El-Said, I., and A. Parman, *Geometric Concepts in Islamic Art*, 1976

Escher, M.C., *Escher on Escher – Exploring the Infinite*, 1986 (compilation of articles from the 1940s and '50s)

Flower, L., *Ideas and Techniques for Fabric Design*, 1987

Ghyka, M., *Geometrical Composition and Design*, 1956

Gillow, N., *William Morris: Designs and Patterns*, 1988

Gimbutas, M., *The Language of the Goddess*, 1989

Glass, F.J., *Drawing, Design and Craftwork*, 1920

Gombrich, E.H., *Illusion in Nature and Art*, 1973; *The Sense of Order*, 1979

Gregory, R.L., *Eye and Brain: The Psychology of Seeing*, 1966

Grillo, P.J., *Form, Function and Design*, 1975

Haeckel, E., *Art Forms in Nature*, 1974 (first published 1904)

Horemis, S., *Optical and Geometrical Patterns and Designs*, 1970

Jones, O., *The Grammar of Ornament*, 1986 (first published 1856); *The Grammar of Chinese Ornament*, 1987 (first published 1867)

Lewis, P., and G. Darley, *Dictionary of Ornament*, 1990

Locher, J.L., *The World of M.C. Escher*, 1971

Lourie, J., *Textile Graphics / Computer-Aided*, 1973

Meyer, F.S., *Meyer's Handbook of Ornament*, 1987 (first published 1894)

Montgomery, F.M., *Printed Textiles: English and American Cottons and Linens 1700–1850*, 1970

Morris, B., *Liberty Design*, 1989

Munz, L., and G. Kunstler, *Adolf Loos*, 1966

Naylor, G., *The Bauhaus*, 1968

Padwick, R., and T. Walker, *Pattern, Its Structure and Geometry*, 1977

Parry, L., *William Morris*, 1989

Pevsner, N., *An Outline of European Architecture*, 1943; *Pioneers of Modern Design*, 1960

Prisse d'Avennes, A.C.T.E., *The Decorative Art of Arabia*, 1989 (first published 1877)

Reilly, V., *Paisley Patterns*, 1989

Rowe, W., *Original Art Deco Allover Patterns*, 1989

Schoeser, M., *Fabrics and Wallpapers*, 1986

Schoeser, M., and C. Rufey, *English and American textiles*, 1989

Seguy, E.A., *Abstract and Floral Designs*, 1988 (first published 1925)

Shubnikov, A.V., and V.A. Koptsik, *Symmetry in Science and Art*, 1974

Speltz, A., *The Styles of Ornament*, 1959 (first published 1904)

Spies, W., *Victor Vasarely*, 1971

Turner, M., and L. Hoskins, *Silver Studio of Design*, 1988

V&A colour books, *Patterns for Textiles*, 1987; *Designs for Shawls*, 1988; *Novelty Fabrics*, 1988; *Thirties Floral Fabrics*, 1988; *Fifties Furnishing Fabrics*, 1989; *Ikats*, 1989

Verneuil, Ad. and M.P., *Abstract Art Patterns and Designs*, 1988 (first published 1925)

Volbach, W.F., *Early Decorative Textiles*, 1969

Watkinson, R., *William Morris as a Designer*, 1967

Watson, W., *Textile Design and Colour*, third edition 1931

Wilson, E., *Early Medieval Designs*, 1983; *North American Indian Designs*, 1984; *Islamic Designs*, 1988

Wong, W., *Principles of Two-Dimensional Design*, 1972

Yasinskaya, I., *Soviet Textile Design*, 1983

Catalogues

Fashion Institute of Technology, New York, *Ratti and Paisley*, 1986

Middlesex Polytechnic, London, *A Popular Art – British Wallpaper 1930–60*, 1989

Tate Gallery, London, *Warhol*, 1971

Victoria and Albert Museum, London, *Designs for British Dress and Furnishing Fabrics – 18th Century to the Present*, 1986